Glazes for
the Potter

By the same author:

Manual for the Potter
(3rd revised edition)

Glazes for the Potter

William Ruscoe

A Scopas Handbook

Academy Editions · London

St. Martin's Press · New York

Scopas Handbooks

First published in Great Britain
in 1974 by Academy Editions
7 Holland Street London W8

Copyright © 1974 Academy
Editions; all rights reserved.

First published in the U.S.A. in
1974 by St. Martin's Press Inc.,
175 Fifth Avenue New York
N.Y. 10010

Printed and bound in Great Britain
by The Devonshire Press, Torquay

Library of Congress catalog card
number 74-78120

SBN hardback 85670 128 9
SBN paperback 85670 133 5

Contents

Chapter I
Geological origins; earth and fire;
clays and bodies. p.1

Chapter II
Early history of glass and glazed
pottery; types and varieties of
glaze. p.5

Chapter III
Chemical composition of the earth;
glaze composition; glaze components; melting points and
eutectics; fluxes. p.17

Chapter IV
Glaze recipes and molecular
formulae; methods of calculation;
derivation of molecular formulae
from known chemical composition;
formula to recipe; recipe to
formula. p.25

Chapter V
Glaze making from insoluble raw
materials; fritts and fritting. p.35

Chapter VI
Formulating new glazes; selection
from limiting formulae; building
a glaze around different materials;
matt glazes; blending and testing
of glazes. p.45

Chapter VII
Colour in glazes; the colouring
oxides; oxidation and reduction;
kilns and firing. p.56

Chapter VIII
Application of the glaze to the
pottery; decoration and techniques;
glaze tests and faults; kiln packing
and firing control. p.63

Appendix I Atomic weights of
elements used in ceramics. p.79

Appendix II Pottery compounds;
minerals; oxides. p.80

Appendix III Glaze recipes. p.82

List of suppliers. p.86

Bibliography. p.87

Glossary. p.88

v

Preface

The aim in writing this book is to enable potters, at all levels, to make and mix their own glazes, for although excellent glazes can be bought ready-made, far greater knowledge and satisfaction can be achieved by compounding and mixing the raw materials.

In order to keep the book to a reasonable length, I have given only the basic information and have minimised the necessary calculations, while giving enough to enable the artist-potter to make glazes to suit any temperature and to produce work which is individual and personal.

The recipes which are given have all been used or tested, but it is hoped that the book will encourage experiments in the formulation of many others.

My own experiences have been drawn from many sources, from friends and colleagues during fifty years of pottery activities in industry, studio, school and college. Many students and friends have assisted with glaze experiments in England and New Zealand.

I strongly recommend looking at historical examples in our museums as well as further reading; I feel sure that the study of this fascinating subject will not only give increased understanding, but pleasure in the appreciation of qualities and properties which are both technical and artistic.

Making and mixing glazes is an ancient skill and all the technical words have a very precise meaning so I have included a Glossary (p.88) to simplify the text for the beginner.

Acknowledgments
My thanks are due and are offered to the students who have helped in the past with the many glaze experiments. More recently, special thanks to Mrs. Sheila Coldrey, Cowley Manor, Exeter, and to Tom and Joan Allan of New Zealand, for the facilities and help in testing many materials and glazes; to Michael Adams, Librarian at the College of Art, Exeter, for the assistance with the coloured photographs, and to my wife who has greatly assisted me with the drawings and diagrams.

Chapter 1

Geological origins

In order to understand about things made of ceramic materials it is helpful to consider, however briefly, the origins of the earth's crust. It seems certain that great heat, followed by a cooling period was part of its early formation and that change, as well as an ageing process goes on continuously. During the molten stage of the crust the heavier substances tended to settle in layers and as the earth cooled the upper layers solidified and formed igneous rocks. Parts of these rocks, by the processes of change, form sedimentary deposits which themselves become metamorphosed. The thin upper crust is subject to weathering due to exposure to the gaseous atmosphere surrounding the earth, so that rain, heat from the sun, freezing cold, and the movements of the earth, all bring change and a redistribution of substances.

Water brings about geological change by dissolving rocks over great periods of time, washing away the more soluble substances into seas in some regions, and depositing great amounts of fragmented rock, sand and mud in other regions. Enormous quantities of sedimented matter become covered by layers of other sediments; they in turn become gradually compressed by weight and thus, form the sedimentary rocks and clays.

Volcanic action and earthquakes throw up huge masses of rock and lava which are gradually eroded away and deposited as silt in oceans and lakes. From all this activity over millions of years we have beds of disintegrated and decomposed rock from which soluble matter has been washed away to leave us with clay and other deposits. Soluble matter may emerge as the dried up beds of ancient seas or lakes.

Earth and fire

Clay and heat are the prerequisites of the potter, followed by glass or glaze, and the discovery that clay could be hardened by fire may be as old as the discovery of fire itself. Much later man discovered, through a combination of accident and experience, that a hard glassy substance could also be made by fire and that the two, clay and glass, could be used together as well as separately. We read that the walls of Babylon were made of sun-dried bricks, but in order to protect the walls against the weather, fired and glazed bricks were used together with slabs of stone to face the walls.

With a far greater knowledge than ever before, man is now able to analyse the earth's crust, to explain its make-up and to combine certain elements and natural substances, fusing them together by heat into artifacts of usefulness and beauty.

After fusion and fairly rapid cooling, some elements produce amorphous glassy substances, which admit the passage of light, while others are crystalline and diffract light, and still others are opaque and reflect light. Obsidian, a black glass formed by volcanic action, is an example of glass formed by natural processes and recent instances of nuclear test explosions fusing desert sands indicate that when the right ingredients are brought together with sufficient heat then glassy substances are obtained.

Clays and bodies

The term *body* is used to describe mixtures of clays and other materials and some knowledge of these is important as they provide the structure and form of the pot. Glaze is used to coat or cover the pot and to enhance its beauty or to make it less porous and more hygienic. Both glaze and clay have to be compatible when united by fire, as problems of expansion and contraction occur and the correct heat treatment is of paramount importance.

Unless one is seeking and mining clay and going through all the processes of preparation, it is better to obtain clay and body from suppliers of reliable materials who provide information concerning their properties.

Suitable glazes will also be available to fit particular bodies, but it is much more interesting to be able to compound one's own glazes, and ready ground glaze materials can be purchased as easily as prepared glazes. Suppliers of glaze materials provide equipment and kilns as well as much information regarding their use, but will not give the recipes of their prepared glazes.

Natural clays are generally classified or named according to the location in which they are found. The main types are; ball clay, china clay, fireclay and red or brown clay.

Ball clays, sometimes called black or blue clays, are often of that colour when freshly mined, firing to a creamy-white. Found in Devon and Dorset and other parts of the world, they are very plastic, and for this reason are seldom used alone. Ball clays vary considerably; some mature at fairly low temperatures, others at stoneware heats. When used alone they do not dry well and warp while shrinking, but mixed with other materials they form the foundation for earthenware and other bodies.

China clay, or kaolin, has very little plasticity and is seldom used alone. Regarded as the purest and whitest form of clay, it is usually used when clay is needed in glazes and it also gives whiteness and translucency to porcelain and china. It is found in the south-west of England as well as other parts of the world.

Fireclays are not fully classified, but as the name implies, they resist heat and are used for the linings of kilns and furnaces of all kinds. They are plastic and buff-coloured when fired. Often used by artist-potters in the production of stoneware, they contain considerable amounts of iron. Fireclays are found in the Midlands and Scotland near the coal seams.

Red or brown clays are found in widespread locations, and are impregnated with iron, which gives their characteristic red, brown or yellow colour. Their plasticity is good, but their firing range is low, partly due to their iron content. Large quantities of these clays outcrop on the earth's surface and much of the early pottery was made from them.

Bodies are compounded for various reasons, usually to achieve hardness, whiteness or translucency. The natural clays, though forming the foundation for bodies, have to be refined and purified, chiefly by having the iron particles removed as these give colour and specks. Other materials such as flint, stone and felspars and in the case of china, bone ash, are added to complete the body.

Grog is previously fired pottery crushed and ground into particles of various sizes, which are passed through screens and added to the clay or body. It is used to give texture and to assist in drying and firing.

Chamotte is a similar addition, except that fired powdered clay is used as the body or clay admixture. Both help to reduce shrinkage and warping.

Firing techniques of clay, body and glaze
The temperature range limits of a particular type of kiln will determine what sort of clay, body and glaze are to be used as well as the technique of firing. Technically it is possible to fire all components at the same time, but often this is not practical. At least two firings are usual; the first a slow firing to change the clay into the biscuit state and a second firing which may be quicker, to fuse the glaze.

Stoneware and porcelain are usually fired to a soft biscuit (950°C) and after the glaze is applied, fired again to the maturing temperature of body and glaze (1250–1300°C).

Earthenware and china are fired to a hard biscuit state and then glazed and fired again at lower temperatures. This technique enables the body to be supported during the biscuit fire, but as the hard biscuit is not so porous the glaze is a little more difficult to apply. The biscuit fire for earthenware is about 1150–1200°C., and for china, 1300°C. The glaze fire for either is 1050°C.

Red and brown clays can be treated by either technique and can have softer glazes. The temperature limits are about 1100°C. In all cases the biscuit firing must be slower than the glaze fire in order to eliminate steam, as water in a combined state is present in clays up to the temperature of red heat, 500°C.

Chapter II

Early history of glass and glazed pottery

In the Near East the earliest evidence found of glass-making dates from about 4000 BC, and glaze recipes were recorded on fired clay tablets in about 2000 BC. Early glass and glaze-making would have been empirical and keeping records was important. Objects made of glass were regarded as precious and ways must soon have been found to use glass in coating pottery vessels. The turquoise colour of the wares, due to the presence of copper, indicates an alkaline glaze and the desert sands made fusible by additions of soda and potash provided the necessary ingredients. This richly coloured glass was probably first melted, cooled and crushed, then melted again to assist fusion and to make it workable. In this manner a fritt would have formed and as the crucibles for melting the glass became coated with a hard glaze, so the method was discovered for covering pottery vessels.

The highly alkaline glass and glazes of these early days were not entirely satisfactory as they tended to decompose and to peel off the pottery. The addition of calcium was needed to prevent solubility and more complex mixtures were slowly evolved.

The discovery of lead as a glaze material was an important factor in this development, as were the opacifying qualities of tin. The latter enabled a hard white glaze to be made which covered up the sandy coloured clay and gave the ceramic a white appearance and which in turn gave a foundation for bright colours. Knowledge of glass and glazes spread and the use of the opaque glaze became common throughout the Middle East and later in Europe.

Across the Mediterranean the ancient Greek potters developed their own particular type of glossy finish to their ceramics. The red clay was painted with a shiny black pigment and was sometimes painted with the white colour, creating an effective contrast, between the black and white glazes and the terracotta pottery. This black pigment defied analysis until researches by Dr. Theodore Schumann in Germany during the second world war revealed its chemistry. The Romans also used red clays with an alkaline glaze, which gave a lustrous rich red shine to their Samian ware.

The Medieval western world moved on to the use of simple, yet effective lead glazes. In some cases the potters merely dusted the damp surface of the pot with galena, a lead ore which combined during firing with the silica of the clay.

1. Stoneware bowl in off-white glaze with painted iron and scratched decoration. The flecks of colour are from particles of iron in the clay; reduction firing at 1300°C. By William Ruscoe

In Germany and Flanders a unique vapour glaze was developed. At stoneware temperatures of about 1200°C., common salt was thrown into the furnace. The salt vapourised at the intense heat and the sodium part of the vapour settled on the surface of the ceramic combining with the silica of the clay to form a sodium silicate, which in itself is a glassy substance. This simple operation was often a closely guarded secret, but the knowledge of it spread to England where it became one of the methods of glazing. Competition from softer glazes and other types of pottery may have led to its decline, although it is still in use today for certain types of ceramic wares.

Knowledge of the lead and alkaline glazes and the use of tin, developed in the Near East, spreading throughout the entire Islamic world and via Spain into Europe. The opaque glaze provided a suitable background for rich colours, as well as a foundation glaze for the lustre painting invented by the Persians and developed into a fine art by their painters and those of Spain and Italy. The Italians used it to cover the ceramic sculptures of the Della Robbia family. Tin-enamelled wares were known as Majolica, Hispano-Moresque, faience, and in Holland as Delft. The Dutch potters of the town of Delft found that the opaque glaze suited the blue colour from cobalt and they almost abandoned the yellow, green and purple of the Majolica painters, in favour of cobalt. The term Delft-ware became a generic name for wares of this type made in England and elsewhere.

In remote China, lead glazes were in use quite early in the history of ceramics, and high temperature glazes were soon developed. These glazes were felspathic in nature and were unique to the Far East. Knowledge of them spread outwards through the mainland and to Korea and Japan. Developments of this nature depend on the discovery of the necessary raw materials and China had rich deposits of kaolin and petunze which would only require the addition of limestone to provide calcium as a flux and other active fluxes were obtainable from the ashes of wood. Accidental glazing of the shoulders of pots where the ashes settled during firing would suggest a direct use of this valuable source of alkali. These fine hard glazes on stoneware and porcelain were envied and emulated by other races.

Some peoples never made ceramics, others only got as far as unglazed wares. The pre-Columbian pottery of America falls into this category, as does also the pottery of central Africa. In some cases a polish was achieved by rubbing the surface of the wares with haematite or the roots of trees, to give a waxy finish.

The spread of knowledge from the Far East stopped short in the Pacific, but in Fiji an interesting glass-like finish was produced by taking the pottery from the fire while fairly hot and rubbing the surface with a resinous gum. The heat melted the gum and this easy method of application sealed the porous surface, covering it with a smooth polish. These finishes are not glazes but they indicate the universal need to render the pottery impervious to moisture and dirt.

Types and varieties of glazes
The study of glazes can be approached in many ways. Classification by the nature of the materials, or by temperature alone can indicate the type. The place of origin, with the geological background and the manner in which they are used, whether raw, fritted, or as vapour glaze, all give some aspect of their use. Glazes are often identified by

certain colour effects, but all have basically the same chemical make-up and eventually the trail leads back to the geological origins.

Alkaline glazes

These glazes, used for centuries by the Egyptians, Persians and others, display a softness of appearance together with characteristic strong bright colours, but they are liable to craze and to become fluid when over-fired. These tendencies are due to the active nature of the fluxes, soda and potash, which are present.

At high temperatures the felspars, themselves natural fritts, provide the required soda-potash fluxes, but at the same time introduce high amounts of silica.

The well-known turquoise and blue from copper and cobalt have colour value and intensity. Iron and manganese also give rich colouration, suitable for decorative wares when strong colours are needed.

Ash glazes

From the earliest days of glass-making, the ashes from burnt wood and other plants have been used in assisting the glass-forming minerals. When vegetable matter is burnt, there remains the ash, the non-combustible matter, which is rich in potash, lime, alumina and silica, as well as traces of other glass-forming agents and colourants. Unfortunately, ashes vary considerably between different plants from different areas as chemical analysis reveals, and modern glass-makers usually get all their supplies of glass-forming substances from minerals. However, the individual potter and glazer can use any supply of wood or vegetable ash which may be available. It can be used alone, experimentally and the ash from clean grass cuttings may produce astonishing results on a body rich in silica, such as porcelain, the colour derived from built-in traces of metallic oxides.

Most users of ash suggest that a mixture of 40% ash, 40% felspar and 20% clay be used, but blends of varying amounts, with less clay, also yield good results. To prepare the ash for use it is usual to soak it in a plentiful supply of water for a day or so. The excess water will contain some soluble soda, potash, etc., and will be somewhat caustic. The lye water is poured away and the wet ash dried and sieved ready for weighing and use.

Aventurine glazes

These are amorphous glazes in which the separation of isolated crystals produces the appearance of spangles suspended in the glass

8

2. Reduced lustre painting and aventurine glaze, made by Pilkingtons.
Collection of B. Harris

which resembles the mineral aventurine. A heavy saturation of iron
helps to form the small crystals, but other factors and colours are
affected by the use of boric oxide in fritted form. Soda-potash and
lead-based glazes firing at about 1000°C. can take 20% of iron
spangles to achieve saturation.

Bristol glazes

The so-called Bristol glazes, named after the place of their origin,
are regarded as middle range oxidised stoneware glazes. They were
developed to eliminate the use of lead in its raw state by the use of
zinc, but since lead may now be obtained in a safer form by fritting,
Bristol glazes are somewhat superseded. Other fluxes usually make-
up the bases; lime and potash cut down the use of too much zinc so
that glossy or matt glazes may be achieved.

Celadon

This well-known coloured glaze, bearing the name of an eighteenth-
century French actor who wore clothes of this colour, was produced

in China on stoneware and porcelain and was greatly esteemed. Possibly inspired by jade, which some of the colours closely resemble, celadons are dependent on a small percentage of iron being present in the glaze (normally 1 to 3%) and on being fired in a strong reducing atmosphere.

The colour varies between different localities, due, perhaps, to variations in materials used and to the degree of reduction achieved. This large class of single-colour glazes produced an astonishing variety of cool sea-greens, blue-greens and grey-greens. Made in most parts of China, Korea, Japan and South Eastern Asia; the glaze is usually enhanced by decorative carving or incised lines in the body of the wares, which cause the glaze to pool in varying depths and intensity of colour.

Other iron-stained glazes

When the amounts of iron are increased in felspathic glazes the cool, pale celadon colour is lost and dark grey-browns to black emerge, with rust colour breaking through when the glaze becomes saturated with metal. These rust to black glazes, again of great variety, may have originated from the same source as celadon: iron-bearing earth and rock fluxed with the ashes of plants and baked in high temperature furnaces in which reduction was readily attainable at temperatures around the 1250 to 1350°C. range, with quantities of iron reaching 10 to 15%.

Effects known as hares fur, tea dust, oil spots, tenmoku, tessha and kaki are all produced by iron-stained glazes, some being the result of over-saturation which causes undissolved particles to break through the surface of the glaze.

Chun glazes

These coloured glazes were the forerunners of the copper red glazes of the Chinese. Produced on a light, buff coloured stoneware, they are essentially opalescent, the glaze being tinted a pale lavender-blue with reddish purple splashes. Much has been written about the mysteries of early Chinese glazes and in particular on how the bluish opalescence was achieved with a seeming contradiction of copper red and blue colour on the same piece. It now seems to be established that the lavender colour is due to a small amount of iron, and the reddish purple to splashes of copper in a colloidal state, well dispersed in the glaze.

3. Jug in stoneware, brown-black glaze
with rust decoration, reduction firing
at130°C. By William Ruscoe

The opalescence is considered to be due to the presence of phos-
phorus, possibly inherent or introduced in the form of bone-ash. A
reducing fire would develop the colours in various degrees and analysis
shows the presence of tin or titanium, but as we do not know the
actual materials from which these glazes were made, only the chemical

11

composition can be established. Many of the qualities and variations of old Chinese glazes may be due to the fact that traces of minerals in the raw materials, so called impurities, would vary from different sources.

Copper red glazes

The use of copper in metal and ceramic work is continuous and colourful, as it is a source of many colours when used in different glazes and under varying conditions of firing. It is nevertheless sometimes difficult to use alone owing to its elusive and volatile nature. In the realms of high temperature, and in felspathic glazes, fired in a reducing atmosphere, the resulting copper oxide or carbonate takes on the colour of the metal. The glaze can be anything from a dirty grey to a liver-red, but at its best coppery- and blood-reds emerge. The stimulating red requires little reduction and the right ingredients in the glaze, together with the correct amount of copper, (usually 0.5%) produces the desired colour.

Many artists and scientists in the past have researched and produced good copper reds, but to the individual potter it still remains a challenge. There is a good deal of mystery as to how the Chinese produced their copper reds with apparent ease and certainty, although, judging by the rarity of the wares, there does not seem to be a lot of it about in the western world.

Varieties of copper stained glazes are known as: '*sang de boeuf*', 'peach-bloom' and '*flambe*'. Regarded as furnace transmutations, streaks of purple, grey and blue as well as red and green can be effected. The precious peach-bloom which is a pinkish red is often broken by flecks of green and brown, mottled or in patches of colour.

Crackle glazes

Crackle glazes are usually opaque and seldom coloured, although they can be so treated. They were much appreciated by the Chinese, who it seems turned a defect of crazing into a decorative crackle of controllable mesh. It is certain that the cracking of the glaze was deliberately sought and colour was rubbed into the cracks in order to enhance the pattern or mesh of lines. A fine, close crackle or a widely spaced set of cracks was possible and often other decorations were added or painted on the surface.

Spacing of cracks in a glaze can be achieved by using materials with a high rate of expansion and contraction when heated. By increasing or decreasing the amounts of these substances in the glaze

4. Porcelain bowl with crackle glaze, painted iron decoration; reduction firing at 1300°C. By William Ruscoe

it is possible to have some control over the spacing. The following table shows the effects on cracks on a glazed porcelain body, when the mixtures are varied.

Potash felspar	Cornish stone	China clay	Mixed to produce
55%	35%	10%	fine cracks
55%	33%	12%	wider cracks
55%	30%	15%	wide cracks

These cracks also vary according to the thickness of the glaze deposited on the pot and many cracks appear immediately on cooling while others are delayed for some time. Stain can be induced into the lines at different times.

Crystalline glazes

Matt glazes depend on minute crystals evenly distributed for a smooth uniform appearance. Crystal glazes have large, visible crystals deliberately sought and controlled to appear in the right place. Many factors have to be considered in order to achieve the beautiful star-like effects and slow cooling of the kiln after reaching the maturing temperature is necessary in order to allow the crystals to grow. The composition of the glaze should have little or no alumina, and a large proportion of zinc introduced with soda, lead and boron as fluxes. Other oxides may be used to give a high saturation of crystal forming agents, such as titanium oxide, rutile, and vanadium oxide, as well as those providing colour.

Natural glazes

Some natural clays, loams and rocks make glazes, with or without an admixture, when fused at high temperatures around 1280°C. and on stoneware bodies. The clays have some fluxes in them, such as about 5% iron, some manganese and titanium oxides. On account of these colouring oxides they yield brown glazes, suitable for coarse stonewares. Fusible clays are rarely used alone as they are liable to be irregular in composition and since by analysis and synthesis they can be adjusted to suit firing conditions by adding extra fluxes.

Glazes made from rocks and minerals which contain fluxes are more useful if a colourless glaze is required. The felspars are examples of natural fritts, but again extra fluxes may be needed to bring down the fusion point and these can easily be added when the composition of the materials are known by analysis.

Volcanic rocks, basalt, lava, ashes and pumice yield impure substances varying between glassy obsidian and a fine dust, which can be of use alone or as admixtures when dark coloured glazes are being produced. Most of these substances contain iron in large amounts which has fluxing powers as well as being a colourant at high temperatures.

Salt glaze

This type of glossy finish is produced by the vapourised action of common salt on the surface of ceramic wares at temperatures of about 1200°C. Usually the glazing is done at a single firing and at the height of the fire when the salt is introduced into the kiln by means of the fire mouths or other openings. The salt is decomposed by the heat and volatile vapours of sodium oxide and hydrochloric acid are

5. A group of salt-glazed stoneware by the Martin Brothers, etched and coloured with oxides. Author's collection

formed. The sodium combines with the silica and alumina of the clay to form a thin, vitrified glassy coating not only on the ware but also on the brickwork of the kiln, and for this reason special furnaces are used for salt-glazing. Electric kilns are unsuitable as the heating elements would be adversely affected.

Its hard, vitreous surface makes it suitable for drain-pipes and chemical wares and a few artist-potters have also found it aesthetically pleasing and capable of great beauty. Although not usually considered as a coloured glaze it may be used on coloured clays or over coloured dips or washes. The early brown wares have a rough texture, but the white salt-glazed wares of Staffordshire have a smoother glaze and in some cases vie with porcelain in refined finish.

This very simple form of glazing lingered on in country potteries making utilitarian brown stoneware during the nineteenth century, while a revival of individualistic coloured wares of decorative value continued in London with the work of the Martin Brothers. This unique type of stoneware glaze has qualities quite unlike any other kind of ceramic and is becoming popular again with individual potters in various parts of the world.

15

Raku glazes

The making of Raku is a form of ritualistic pottery-making origina-ting from the Japanese tea ceremony as far back as the 16th century, the custom being associated with the philosophy of Zen. The ceremonious making, baking and glazing of the tea bowls made for the occasion exemplified the simple and natural beauty of the earth, fashioned by man and glazed and fired at the same time. The process could be seen to happen in a short period of time. The melting of the glaze in an open kiln might be watched and the withdrawal of the pot and its sudden cooling gave a simple demonstration of the complexities of a creative craft.

The kilns erected on the spot or brought on the backs of itinerant potters, were only capable of low temperatures of about 750–950°C., and the clay used was coarse and mixed with sand or grog to with-stand the thermal shock of rapid heating and cooling. After the bis-cuit firing the pot was glazed and placed in a hot furnace, the heat was raised a little while the glaze melted and then the pot was with-drawn with tongs, to be rapidly cooled in water, charcoal or sawdust. Oxidation and reduction would take place and colouring oxides, apart from colour in the clay, would also play their part.

Glazes of simple eutectic mixtures of lead and silica fuse at about 750°C., and small additions of clay would help the glaze to adhere to the pot. The compositions in the following table fuse easily.

Mixture	Lead oxide	Flint or quartz	Temp. °C.
$2\ PbO\ SiO_2$	$PbO\ 88\cdot1\%$	$SiO_2\ 11\cdot9\%$	746
$PbO\ SiO_2$	$PbO\ 78\cdot7\%$	$SiO_2\ 21\cdot3\%$	770

As raw lead is toxic it would be safer to use the lead in a fritted form. Other fritts, such as Wenger soft alkaline or soft borax, can be used with about 5% of clay to help the glaze adhere.

Chapter III

Chemical composition of the earth

We may not know how the earth was formed or from whence it came, but we do know a lot about its chemical make-up. Scientists have solved a lot of the secrets of the earth's crust and by analysis they have determined the elements of its composition and of its atomic structure.

Heavier substances tend to sink in a molten amalgam, so it follows that some elements are heavier than others. These elements seldom exist alone, but are mainly mixed up by the forces of nature into compounds and mixtures of varying substances, solids, liquids and gases, differing greatly in quantity and distribution over the earth's surface.

It is essential to differentiate between an element and a compound in order to understand something about the various minerals, oxides and other mixtures.

An element is defined as a substance which so far as is known contains only one kind of atom: an atom regarded as the smallest particle of an element which can take part in a chemical change. The atoms of the different elements have greatly differing weights, known as the atomic weights (abbreviated to At. Wts.) and these weights are based on the lightest of all the elements, hydrogen, which is symbolised by its first letter H. and given the atomic weight of 1. Symbols are used to avoid writing Latin and other names, thus a heavy element, lead, is symbolised by Pb., for plumbum and its atomic weight is 207, which means that one atom of lead is 207 times heavier than one atom of hydrogen. Science has established the comparative weights of the known elements and there are about 100 of them, but the glaze-maker needs only to be concerned with less than half of these (see Appendix I) .

A compound is a substance which is composed of more than one kind of element, combined in definite proportions and as atoms are involved these groups are called molecules. Molecules are the units which make up matter and a molecule may be regarded as the smallest particle existing separately in a compound. Molecular weights are the combined weights of the atoms in its structure. An example is given to explain this: water has a formula of H_2O, where the small $_2$ below the line indicates two atoms of hydrogen to one atom of oxygen.

The At. Wt. of hydrogen, H is 1, therefore 2 atoms = 2
The At. Wt. of oxygen, O is 16, therefore 1 atom = 16
                                                        ——
The molecular weight of water, H_2O,   = 18

When a substance has several different compounds in its make-up the weights of the various compounds must be added together to give the formula weight, usually named the combined or molecular weight (abbreviated to Mol.Wt.). Should there be more molecules of one compound than another, then a figure indicating this is written above the base line in front of the molecule it refers to, for example; china clay has a formula $Al_2O_3. 2SiO_2. 2H_2O$; its formula or molecular weight being 258. This is arrived at by using the following method.

Al_2 (i.e. 2 atoms of aluminium) $= 27 \times 2 =$ 54
O_3 (i.e. 3 atoms of oxygen) $\quad = 16 \times 3 =$ 48
                                                        ——
$\qquad\qquad\qquad\qquad\qquad\qquad\quad 102 \times 1\,\text{Mol.} = 102$

$2\begin{cases}Si & \text{(i.e. 1 atom of silicon)} & = 28 \times 1 = & 28 \\ O_2 & \text{(i.e. 2 atoms of oxygen)} & = 16 \times 2 = & 32\end{cases}$
                                                        ——
$\qquad\qquad\qquad\qquad\qquad\qquad\quad 60 \times 2\,\text{Mol.} = 120$

$2\begin{cases}H_2 & \text{(i.e. 2 atoms of hydrogen)} & = 1 \times 2 = & 2 \\ O & \text{(i.e. 1 atom of oxygen)} & = 16 \times 1 = & 16\end{cases}$
                                                        ——
$\qquad\qquad\qquad\qquad\qquad\qquad\quad 18 \times 2\,\text{Mol.} = 36$
                                                        ——

The molecular weight of china clay, $Al_2O_3 . 2SiO_2 . 2H_2O$ is 258

The minerals and materials which are gathered from the earth's crust are analysed by ceramic chemists for their usefulness in glaze making. The suppliers of glaze-making materials may publish the formulae of their products, but it is necessary for the glaze-maker to be able to read the published formulae so that the component parts of a glaze may be correctly assembled, (see Appendix II).

Students of chemistry will be familiar with the facts and the methods of calculation, those unfamiliar with such knowledge will need to be able to read the abbreviated symbols and to understand how the Mol.Wts. are arrived at.

The reason for this is that the molecular parts of a glaze have to be multiplied by the molecular weights of the materials used, in order to assemble the correct amounts of the components. Ability to do the necessary arithmetic is essential. To the uninitiated, formulae can look bewildering, but by understanding the limits of their usefulness much time can be saved.

Until about a century ago, the glaze compositions in use were the results of years of trial and error and of the chance observation of accidental happenings with the materials used. Great secrecy surrounded the knowledge of certain materials. The concept of molecular formulae for glazes, mainly due to Dr. Hermann Seger, showed that the mysterious ingredients follow rules which were unknown previously.

It was found in the past that certain oxides of sodium and potassium have the power of lowering the melting point of silica, which is the chief glass-forming substance. Other bases were found with different fluxing powers and the proportions of flux to the heat-resisting silica were worked out by trial and error. Although silica alone will make a glass it would not melt at the temperatures possible with primitive furnaces, but when mixed with fluxes, glass and glazes were feasible.

Later, a stabiliser in the form of a little clay was added to the melt, to prevent the sudden melting and running of the glaze. So the Base Amphoteric Acid combination was arrived at, having an enormous number of possible variations giving different glazes to suit temperatures of a wide range.

Glaze composition

Glazes are composed to fit the bodies and to suit the temperatures at which the potter may wish to work. The behaviour of the glaze under heat is affected by its composition as well as by the atmosphere of the kiln, whether oxidising or reducing. The range of temperature is also important, a wide fusion range being better than a sharp one.

As glaze materials, in common with most earthly materials, are combined with oxygen, the oxides play an important part in glaze composition. Oxygen is prevalent in the atmosphere, in water, and is also necessary for combustion. It combines readily with other elements—the rusting of iron is a familiar example of oxidation.

Glazes when fired are oxides (although some carbonates may enter into the raw composition) and they are expressed as formulae, recipes, or by chemical composition. When expressed as a formula, the basic or fluxing oxides are arranged on the left and are taken to represent $1 \cdot 0$, the acids on the right and the amphoteric or neutral groups in the middle. R represents the metal and O the oxygen.

Proportions of bases amphoterics or acids, are variable within the limits. The amphoteric is usually one tenth to one sixth in ratio to the acids.

In the following table typical formulae for various ceramics are expressed as alumina-silica ratios.

Bases R O	Amphoteric R_2O_3	Acids $R O_2$	Temp.°C.	Type	Usage
1·0	0·1–0·5	1·2–3·5	850–1150	Raw	Earthenware
1·0	0·2–0·9	2·0–7·0	1150–1300	Raw	Stoneware
1·0	0·5–1·2	4·0–12·0	1300–1500	Raw	Porcelain
1·0	0·1–0·6	2·0–4·0	1000–1200	Fritted	Earthenware
1·0	0·1–0·6	2·0–4·5	1000–1200	Fritted	China and soft Porcelain

These formulae cover a wide field. The number of glazes which could be formulated are many and varied, especially when the bases within the unified RO are considered.

Bases Lead oxide may be used as a single base, but it is usual to use more than one base and the more bases used will produce a more fusible glaze. In order of fluxing powers the bases are: lithium oxide, lead oxide, sodium oxide, potassium oxide, barium oxide, calcium oxide, strontium oxide, magnesium oxide and zinc oxide. In the formula of a glaze the bases must always have total unity. The limits of the bases must also be seen in terms of temperatures. In general, the use of lead ceases at 1200°C., to be replaced at higher temperatures by the less active fluxes such as calcium, magnesium and barium. Potash and soda are used throughout the range, as well as small amounts of zinc which assist the other oxides to fuse. Zinc may also be used in fairly large amounts from about 1160°C. There are, of course, many exceptions to all these rules, depending on the qualities being sought in the glaze.

Amphoteric This is alumina, usually present in glazes up to 18 per cent, but considerably less in glass. It is obtained by using clay, but it is also present in many minerals used by the glaze-maker.

Acids Silica is the chief acidic oxide for clay, glass and glaze. It can be obtained in a free state or in combination with other minerals.

Boric oxide Is more fusible than silica and it is a glass forming substance. Its fluxing powers enable it to be used in low temperature glazes. It is usually grouped in the amphoteric column. Its use decreases the temperature required to fuse a glaze, whereas alumina and silica require more heat as the ratios are increased.

Limiting formulae can only be used as approximate guides and the potter would be unwise to rely solely on these, but they do provide a starting point to be proved by trial and adjustment.

Glazes are usually referred to as either raw or fritted: these are important differences which control the use of many materials. Raw glazes are those made from raw materials which do not dissolve in water. Fritted glazes involve the use of soluble materials which have been rendered insoluble by being melted together in a special furnace called a fritt kiln. Classification is sometimes expressed in terms of the basic fluxes used and alkaline, lead or leadless are indicative names giving a clue to the principal base.

Glaze components: melting points and eutectics

In order to understand how certain glaze components affect each other in lowering or raising melting points, it is helpful to examine a few eutectic mixtures of substances and their reaction under heat. Mixtures of oxides usually have lower melting points than single oxides. Different proportions of oxides give different results, but the proportions of two oxides which give the lowest melting point is the eutectic mixture. Eutectics are important in glaze composition,

6. Group of high temperature wares, showing cut-glaze decoration, brush painting and crackle glaze. 1300°C. By William Ruscoe

although somewhat unstable, they have a definite chemical composition, a sharp melting point and being easily decomposed.

The fact that combinations of materials tend to have a lower melting point than when used singly is the basic premise of glaze-making as this tendency enables refractory substances to be used and combined with other, less heat-resisting materials. It is strange, but true, that combinations of interacting substances under heat give lower melting points than any of the constituents, as will be seen by the following table.

Substance		Melting pt.	Percentage	Melting pt. of Mixture
Lead oxide	PbO	876	PbO 78·7	770°C
Silica	SiO$_2$	1700	SiO$_2$ 21·3	
Lead oxide	PbO	876	PbO 91·7	552°C
Lead orthosilicate	2PbO.SiO$_2$	746	SiO$_2$ 8·3	

Much may be learned about fusion and melting points by experimentation. An example is potash felspar, in itself a eutectic mixture, which melts alone at 1220°C., but which will stand additions of silica, melting point 1700°C., without raising the temperature too much.

An example is given where the ratio of potash felspar to silica is 1:2.

Substance	Molecular comp.	Percentage comp.	Meltg pt.
1 part of potash felspar	K$_2$O. Al$_2$O$_3$. 6SiO$_2$	13·8 K$_2$O 15·0 Al$_2$O$_3$ 71·2 SiO$_2$	1285°C
2 parts of silica	2SiO$_2$		

Other ratios of 1:3 or 1:6 only raise the melting point by 20°C. or 30°C.

In a similar way, whiting which does not fuse at 1250°C., when mixed in the proportion of 1 to 3 with potash felspar, will melt into a glassy substance at this temperature.

There are many instances of eutectics which cannot be given here, but it is sufficient to realise that melting is brought about by the interaction of various oxides within the glaze when subjected to heat.

The fusion point of a glaze may be lowered or raised by various means. To lower the fusion point, decrease the amounts of silica and alumina in the glaze, adding more active fluxes such as lead, soda, potash, zinc or boric oxide, while at the same time decreasing the less active fluxes: lime, magnesium and barium.

The use of fritts instead of raw materials will also help fusion, when they can replace the appropriate oxides. To raise the fusion point of a glaze, increase the silica and alumina, and in general reverse the lowering procedures.

Fluxes, and the interaction of various oxides

Fluxes may be regarded as substances which when mixed with another, more refractory, substance, lower the melting point of the latter. Thus lime and other basic substances are fluxes when added to silica and conversely, silica is a flux when added to lime or other bases. Although the basic fluxes rely on the interaction of silica and other oxides, they do have individual characteristics and behave differently at various temperatures. An important difference is the way in which the colouring oxides, which also have some fluxing power, respond to the basic fluxes. Some fluxes are more powerful and active than others and in the range of firing they vary considerably.

Lead oxide PbO, is an active flux, which can be used alone or with other bases up to 1200°C., beyond which point it volatilizes. Although it is obtainable as a free base it should be used in a fritted form on account of its poisonous nature.

Potassium and sodium oxides K_2O and Na_2O are usually classed together. When used alone as bases, crazing often results due to the high expansion under heat and therefore, contraction upon cooling. When used as free bases they require fritting due to solubility. They are obtainable in an insoluble form from felspars (natural fritts) and they can be used over the entire range of temperatures. Both are potent fluxes giving the characteristic colour-responses of alkaline glazes.

Calcium oxide (lime) CaO, *magnesium oxide* MgO and *barium oxide* BaO, are alkaline earths which are less active at low temperatures but become increasingly potent at high temperatures. Their effectiveness begins about 1060°C., and all are obtainable as free bases or combined with other substances. Good colour effects are obtained in high temperature glazes.

Zinc oxide ZnO, is a useful flux in small or large amounts. It can be obtained in a free form but it is best used in a calcined form and greatly assists the fusion of other oxides. Its effectiveness begins at about 1060°C., and it can be used for higher temperatures. Zinc oxide was used to replace lead in Bristol glazes.

Lithium oxide Li_2O, acts in a similar way to sodium, but it is seldom used as it is more expensive. It is obtainable in a free and insoluble form and can be used as lithium carbonate.

Strontium oxide SrO, is similar to calcium, but as calcium is cheap and strontium expensive, calcium is commonly used as whiting.

Boric oxide B_2O_3 is a powerful flux and low temperature glazes can be made with it. Most sources of boric oxide are soluble and it is usual to use borax fritts when introducing this widely used flux. Colemanite enables boric oxide to be used in an insoluble form but this also introduces some calcium at the same time; like potassium and sodium, boric oxide can be used over the entire temperature range.

Lead-boro-silicate glazes are widely used for tablewares.

Chapter IV

Glaze recipes and molecular formulae; methods of calculation

The recipe of a glaze is an expression of the different proportions of its ingredients, usually in percentage form, for the purpose of weighing out the dry batch.

The molecular formula shows the molecular proportions of the various oxides contained in the ingredients and arranged in the order: R O bases, R_2O_3 amphoterics, R O_2 acids; R representing the metal and the R O portion taken as unity. In this manner a lead glaze formula would be written, $PbO. 0.2 Al_2O_3. 1.75 SiO_2$. This expressed as a recipe might read:

white lead	65.0	parts by weight
china clay	13.5	parts by weight
flint	21.5	parts by weight

The recipe appears to be simple but unrelated at first sight; only by examining its molecular make-up can the relationship be seen. The ingredients of a recipe are usually multiple substances rather than single oxides and as the oxides have to be obtained from whatever source of supply is available they often exist in various forms. For example, other forms of lead might be used, or a lead silicate, and then the recipe would read quite differently.

Alumina is usually obtained by the use of china clay, which also contains silica, but as silica is also necessary the proportions have to be calculated in order that the correct amount is used.

From one formula many different recipes might be devised by using materials from various sources. Conversely, many recipes quite different from each other may be found to have formulae quite similar. For these reasons, comparisons between recipes are rather difficult when they contain a variety of ingredients and constituents. On the other hand, the glaze when represented by formulae is more easily compared and adjusted if necessary.

There is another form in which glazes are expressed, that of percentage chemical composition, which shows the analysis of the glaze into single oxides, but as many of these do not exist in such a convenient form, the percentage chemical composition must be translated into molecular formula and recipe. It is by the multiplication of the molecular parts by the molecular weights that the parts by weight of the recipe are achieved.

No doubt in ancient times and before a knowledge of chemistry was acquired, glazes must have been worked by the empirical method of trial and error. Observation of unusual happenings in the kiln as well as the study of natural phenomena would suggest that certain things might happen if substances were fused together in various proportions. In this way generations of potters might adapt, improve upon and pass on recipes. If supplies of materials changed, varied, or dried up, then a whole set of new tests and experiments would have to be made.

Analytical chemistry and research have made possible the knowledge of the synthesis of glass and glaze-making, so that by using these methods the possibilities of the field are seen. Also, new glass-forming materials have been found in modern times which in turn have widened the scope. It is necessary to know the chemical composition or formula of the substances used and these are usually supplied by the suppliers of glaze materials.

The rules for conversion are well established and the rapid glaze calculator by Colin Pearson and Dennis Healing is recommended to take the tedium out of the necessary calculations.

The calculation of molecular formulae derived from the known percentage composition of materials and glazes

When the quantitative chemical composition of a material or glaze is known, by analysis, it is usually given in percentage form, and as this is not a working recipe it is necessary to formulate it for practical purposes. Assuming that the chemical substances are combined chemically in the material, a formula expressing the atomic and molecular proportions of the constituents can be calculated by the following procedures.

1. Divide the percentage of each chemical by its atomic or molecular weight.

Example: a chemical compound contains potassium (K) 82·98%
oxygen (O) 17·02%

Potassium (K) 82·98÷39 (atomic weight of K)=2·13 atomic parts
Oxygen (O) 17·02÷16 (atomic weight of O)=1·06 atomic parts

2. Reduce the lowest quantity to be obtained by the first rule to the nearest whole number (unity) and divide this into the other quantities to find their ratios.

Taking 1·06 as 1·0 (unity) we find that 2·13÷1·00=2, indicating that there are 2 parts of potassium present to 1 part of oxygen in the compound. Therefore the formula of the compound is K_2O and its formula or molecular weight is 94.

A more complex example of a glaze in percentage chemical composition:

SiO_2 30·23% ÷ Mol. Wt. 60 = 0·504
Al_2O_3 5·87% ÷ Mol. Wt.102 = 0·057
PbO 63·90% ÷ Mol. Wt.223 = 0·287

Applying the second rule, but in this case of a glaze using the base as unity we find:

0·504 ÷ 0·287 (the sum of the base) = 1·75 SiO_2
0·057 ÷ 0·287 (the sum of the base) = 0·20 Al_2O_3
0·287 ÷ 0·287 (the sum of the base) = 1·00 PbO

The formula of the glaze is written, PbO. 0·20 Al_2O_3. 1·75 SiO_2.

Glazes are more often expressed and published as formulae rather than as percentage chemical compositions, as the formula offers a more comparative form and leads through to the recipe. The formula offers easier adjustment should the need arise to adjust the glaze, but the formula must be converted into a working recipe of materials and this requires a further set of calculations.

The calculation of a formula into a recipe for a raw glaze

Proceed as follows and by prior reckoning:
write down the formula to be converted, in this example,

$$PbO. \quad 0·2\ Al_2O_3. \quad 2·0\ SiO_2$$

Draw up a table and at the top of each column indicate the heading allowing a separate column for each oxide contained in the molecular formula of the glaze.

Materials	Mol. Wts.	× Mol. Parts	= Parts by Wt.	Columns for oxides	% Recipe

The parts by weight are determined by multiplying the molecular weights by the molecular parts and the percentage recipe is achieved by converting the parts by weight into percentages thus giving a more convenient form to the parts by weight or recipe.

Firstly deal with the basic oxides, in this case PbO, and enter this in the first column for oxides. From the table of materials used in glazes, choose one which will yield the oxide required. In this case lead oxide (PbO) is selected as it is a single oxide from a raw material. Enter lead oxide in the materials column and 223 in the mol.wts. column. One molecular part will equal 223 parts by weight, enter this under parts by weight and under PbO enter 1·0.

Secondly, china clay will yield Al_2O_3 $2SiO_2$ $2H_2O$. Enter china clay under materials and 258 under mol.wts. As only 0·2 molecular parts are required enter 0·2 under the Al_2O_3 column and 0·4 under SiO_2 as china clay has twice the number of molecules of SiO_2. The H_2O can be disregarded as it burns away, but it is accounted for in the molecular weight of 258. Enter 0·2 in the mol.parts column and multiply by 258 to give 51·6 to be entered in the parts by wt. column.

Thirdly, deal with the SiO_2, as we have chosen flint, but since we already have 0·4 in the SiO_2 column we must deduct this from the required amount of 2·0 which leaves 1·6 to be entered in the SiO_2 column. Enter flint in the materials column, 60 in the mol.wts. column, 1·6 in the mol.parts column and $60 \times 1·6 = 96·0$ in the parts by weight column.

This completes dealing with the oxides and by adding together the parts by weight we have;

Lead oxide	223·0 parts
China clay	51·6 parts
Flint	96·0 parts
	370·6

The parts by weight are each multiplied by 100 and divided by the sum total to give the percentage recipe as follows:

$$\text{Lead oxide} \quad \frac{223·0 \times 100}{370·6} \quad = 60$$

$$\text{China clay} \quad \frac{51·6 \times 100}{370·6} \quad = 14$$

$$\text{Flint} \quad \frac{96·0 \times 100}{370·6} \quad = 26$$

The reason for the recipe in percentage form is that it enables parts of colour or other additives to be more easily proportioned. The completed tables which follow enable the workings to be seen and keeps track of the oxides used as well as checking the totals against the formula to which they must correspond.

7. Stoneware pot, 2 ft. high, off-white glaze with painted iron decoration, reduction firing at 1300°C. By William Ruscoe

Formula: PbO. $0 \cdot 2$ Al$_2$O$_3$. 2 SiO$_2$.

Materials	Mol. Wts.	Mol. Parts.	Parts by Wt.	$1 \cdot 0$ PbO	$0 \cdot 2$ Al$_2$O$_3$	$2 \cdot 0$ SiO$_2$	% Recipe
Lead oxide	223	× $1 \cdot 0$	= $223 \cdot 0$	$1 \cdot 0$			60
China clay	258	× $0 \cdot 2$	= $51 \cdot 6$		$0 \cdot 2$	$0 \cdot 4$	14
Flint	60	× $1 \cdot 6$	= $96 \cdot 0$			$1 \cdot 6$	26
Totals			$370 \cdot 6$	$1 \cdot 0$	$0 \cdot 2$	$2 \cdot 0$	100

29

This method of calculation is the basis by which formulae are converted to recipes, although there are different ways of showing the calculations. A summary of the rules is given:

1. Draw up a table and at the top of each column indicate the heading, allowing a separate column for each oxide contained in the molecular formula of the glaze.

2. From the table of materials used in glazes, choose those which will yield the oxides required. In some cases a single oxide will be obtained from a raw material, and in others, several oxides will form a united part of the material and all must be accounted for, except water or gases which burn away or change. The weights of these are included in the molecular weights.

Materials which contain unwanted oxides cannot be selected.

Soluble substances are only used in fritted glazes.

Proceed by noting the number of molecular parts of the chief oxide required in one molecular part of the raw material.

3. If the required molecular part of an oxide is exceeded by molecular parts in the raw material, divide the required molecular part by this number. This gives the molecular part of the raw materials. For example; if one molecular part of PbO was needed and white lead $2 PbCO_3 . Pb(OH)_2$ mol.wt.776 was chosen, note that this contains 3 molecules of PbO. Therefore only 0·33 molecular parts of white lead should be taken and entered in the table. In any case, lead should always be used in fritted form on account of its toxic nature.

4. Multiply the molecular parts of each oxide in the raw material (disregarding H_2O) by the required molecular parts of the raw material and place the results in the appropriate columns. This shows the molecular parts of the oxides introduced simultaneously.

5. By subtraction note the amounts in molecular parts of those oxides which remain to be accounted for, leaving the alumina and silica until the last.

6. The parts by weight of each raw material are determined by multiplying the molecular parts of the raw materials by their molecular weights. For convenience bring the parts by weight to percentages as colouring oxides are usually added to glazes as percentage parts. Further examples follow showing the use of the foregoing and in practice although some details of subtraction and multiplication may be omitted enough should be tabulated to keep track of the oxides and to check the totals against the formula.

In the two examples which follow, different recipes are derived from the same formula.

Formula $PbO. 0.2 Al_2O_3. 2SiO_2$.

1. When white lead is used, $2PbCO_3. Pb(OH)_2$ Mol.Wt.776 we obtain the following result.

Materials	Mol. Wts.	Mol. Parts	Parts by Wt.	1·0 PbO	0·2 Al_2O_3	2·0 SiO_2	% Recipe
White lead	776	× 0·33	= 258	1·0			64
China clay	258	× 0·20	= 51·6		0·2	0·4	13
Flint	60	× 1·6	= 96·0			1·6	23
Totals			405·6	1·0	0·2	2·0	100

2. When lead sesquisilicate is used $PbO. 1.5 SiO_2$ Mol.Wt.313 we obtain the following result.

Materials	Mol. Wts.	Mol. Parts	Parts by Wt.	1·0 PbO	0·2 Al_2O_3	2·0 SiO_2	% Recipe
Lead sesq	313	× 1·0	= 313	1·0		1·5	84·0
China clay	258	× 0·2	= 51·6		0·2	0·4	14·4
Flint	60	× 0·1	= 6·0			0·1	1·6
Totals			370·6	1·0	0·2	2·0	100·0

The following table is an example of a glaze with two bases potash felspar and whiting.

Formula, $0.5 K_2O \quad 0.6 Al_2O_3. \quad 3.7 SiO_2$
$0.5 CaO$

Materials	Mol. Wts.		Mol. Parts	Parts by Wt.	0·5 K_2O	0·5 CaO	0·6 Al_2O_3	3·7 SiO_2	% Recipe
Potash Fels.	556	×	0·5 =	278·0	0·5		0·5	3·0	72
Whiting	100	×	0·5 =	50·0		0·5			13
China clay	258	×	0·1 =	25·8			0·1	0·2	7
Flint	60	×	0·5 =	30·0				0·5	8
Totals				383·8	0·5	0·5	0·6	3·7	100

The calculation of a recipe or batch into a formula

Although calculations usually follow the 'formula to recipe' method, it is sometimes useful to be able to reverse the process and to convert back a recipe into a formula in order to look into the workings and to compare it with other formulae. This is particularly useful when recipes published without formulae have to be adjusted, which is often the case when recipes do not fit particular bodies or when they do not match up to expectations.

A simple stoneware glaze to fire at 1300°C., is examined. It has a recipe of, 10 parts by weight of china clay

20 parts by weight of whiting

30 parts by weight of flint

40 parts by weight of potash felspar

Draw up a table as follows, placing at the head of the columns for oxides the appropriate ones found in the permanent oxides entering the glaze through the materials. Note that in this case the parts by weight are divided by the mol.wts. of the materials.

Materials	Parts by Wt.	÷	Mol. Wts.	=	Mol. parts	Columns for oxides

The rules for conversion are as follows:

1. Divide the parts by weight of the recipe by the molecular weights of the materials to give the molecular parts.

2. Enter into the separate columns the molecular parts of each permanent oxide introduced by each material, arranged horizontally.

3. Sum up the totals, thus finding the total molecular parts of each permanent oxide.

4. Arrange the quantities in the order of a formula; bases, amphoteric, acid.

5. Add together the bases and divide the quantities by this sum, this gives the formula, with the bases totalling unity.

Commence by dividing the quantity of each material by its mol.wt.

$$
\begin{aligned}
\text{China clay} \quad & 10 \div 258 = 0 \cdot 0387 \\
\text{Whiting} \quad & 20 \div 100 = 0 \cdot 2 \\
\text{Flint} \quad & 30 \div \ 60 = 0 \cdot 5 \\
\text{Potash felspar} \quad & 40 \div 556 = 0 \cdot 0719
\end{aligned}
$$

Arrange in the table. Note that the molecular equivalents of each raw material is multiplied by the quantity of each oxide in its formula: see table of materials.

Materials	Parts by Wt.	Mol. Wts.	Mol. parts	K_2O	CaO	Al_2O_3	SiO_2
China clay	10	÷ 258	= 0·0387			0·0387	0·0774
Whiting	20	÷ 100	= 0·2		0·2		
Flint	30	÷ 60	= 0·5				0·5
Potash fels	40	÷ 556	= 0·0719	0·0719		0·0719	0·4314
				0·0719	0·2	0·1106	1·0088

The sum of the bases is 0·2719, which divided into the other quantities and arranged as a formula gives as follows:

$$\frac{0\cdot0719}{0\cdot2719} = 0\cdot264 \ K_2O$$

$$\frac{0\cdot1106}{0\cdot2719} = 0\cdot4 \ Al_2O_3 \qquad \frac{1\cdot0088}{0\cdot2719} = 3\cdot7 \ SiO_2$$

$$\frac{0\cdot2000}{0\cdot2719} = 0\cdot735 \ CaO$$

This has brought the formula to unity:

0·264 K₂O

   0·4 Al₂O₃ 3·7 SiO₂

0·735 CaO

It should be remembered that the accuracy of the formula depends on the analysis of the materials. It should be regarded as correlated data useful in making comparisons.

Recipe to formula, from a theoretical percentage composition
In this case a recipe of Cornish stone, 85 parts by weight, and whiting, 15 parts by weight, is examined. Temp. 1300°C.
1. A theoretical percentage analysis would be tabulated in the following way:

	K_2O	CaO	Al_2O_3	SiO_2
Cornish stone	7		18	75
Whiting		56		

Disregarding the CO_2 of whiting as this burns away and does not enter the calculations at this stage, it is necessary to multiply the percentage of each oxide found in the materials by the quantities of the recipe and to divide these by 100.

$$K_2O \ \frac{7\times85}{100} = 5\cdot95 \qquad Al_2O_3 \ \frac{18\times85}{100} = 15\cdot30 \qquad SiO_2 \ \frac{75\times85}{100} = 63\cdot75$$

$$CaO \ \frac{56\times15}{100} = 8\cdot40$$

2. Collect the totals of each oxide together and divide them by their molecular weights, in this case;

$$\underset{\text{K}_2\text{O}}{\frac{5 \cdot 95}{94}} = 0 \cdot 063 \quad \underset{\text{CaO}}{\frac{8 \cdot 40}{56}} = 0 \cdot 150 \quad \underset{\text{Al}_2\text{O}_3}{\frac{15 \cdot 30}{102}} = 0 \cdot 150 \quad \underset{\text{SiO}_2}{\frac{63 \cdot 75}{60}} = 1 \cdot 061$$

3. Arrange as a formula, $0 \cdot 063$ K_2O

$$0 \cdot 150 \text{ Al}_2\text{O}_3 \quad 1 \cdot 061 \text{ SiO}_2$$

$$\underline{0 \cdot 150 \text{ CaO}}$$

Total of bases $0 \cdot 213$

4. The above is brought to unity by dividing the total of the bases into each of the bases, alumina, and silica, giving an approximate formula.

$0 \cdot 3$ K_2O

$0 \cdot 7$ Al_2O_3 $5 \cdot 0$ SiO_2

$0 \cdot 7$ CaO

Chapter V

Glaze-making from insoluble raw materials

When glazes are made from materials which do not dissolve in water they are called *raw glazes*. Materials which are soluble in water must be *fritted* first of all to make them insoluble and then mixed with some raw materials to complete the glaze mixture. These are usually referred to as *fritted glazes* meaning glazes which have been rendered insoluble by pre-melting.

Many glazes do not need fritts, but when they are required they may be purchased from suppliers ready made and prepared for use in the same manner as prepared glazes are supplied. The formulae of commercial fritts are usually published.

The individual potter wishing to make his own glazes can do much with insoluble raw materials since many of them are *natural fritts* containing oxides which would otherwise be soluble. The felspars are examples of natural fritts.

There are at least twelve more available raw materials from which raw glazes can be made without recourse to man-made fritts. These are of particular use in the higher range of temperatures, 1100–1300°C., although it is possible by using raw lead to cover the lower range of temperatures also. The raw materials when obtained ready for use should be of the correct particle size and only require the right calculations, weighing out and mixing with water.

It is in this field that stoneware and porcelain glazes can be readily made, using naturally occurring insoluble substances. An example is given for stoneware raw glaze to fire at 1280–1300°C., and the necessary calculations are shown. Consult the list of insoluble substances which follow and use the rules for the calculation of a formula to recipe.

Formula, $0.3 \ K_2O$
$\quad\quad\quad 0.4 \ CaO \quad 0.4 \ Al_2O_3 \quad 3.5 \ SiO_2$
$\quad\quad\quad 0.3 \ BaO$

Materials	Mol. Wts.	Mol. parts.	Parts by Wt.	0.3 K_2O	0.4 CaO	0.3 BaO	0.4 Al_2O_3	3.5 SiO_2	% Recipe
Potash fels.	$556 \times$	$0.3 =$	166.8	0.3			0.3	1.8	43.6
Whiting	$100 \times$	$0.4 =$	40.0		0.4				10.5
Barium carb.	$197 \times$	$0.3 =$	59.1			0.3			15.5
China clay	$258 \times$	$0.1 =$	25.8				0.1	0.2	6.8
Flint	$60 \times$	$1.5 =$	90.0					1.5	23.6
Totals			381.7	0.3	0.4	0.3	0.4	3.5	100.0

RAW MATERIALS

Barium carbonate	China clay	Colemanite	Cornish stone	Cryolite	Dolomite
Felspar potash & Soda	flint (silica)	Magnesium carbonate	Nepheline syenite	Whiting	Zinc Oxide

FRITTS

Alkaline	Borax	Lead bisilicate	Lead sequisilicate	Zircon

OPACIFIERS MATTING AGENTS

Antimony	Tin	Titanium	Zinc	Zirconium

COLORANTS

Chromium	Cobalt	Copper	Iron	Iron chromate	Ilmenite
Manganese	Nickel	Potassium bichromate	Rutile	Uranium	Vanadium

8. Raw materials

9. The two tall pots are 2ft. high in grey-green glazes: the third is 10in. high in white glaze from Cornish stone with cobalt decoration; reduction firing at 1300°C. By William Ruscoe

Insoluble substances for use in raw glazes

Barium carbonate $BaCO_3$ Mol.Wt.197

Used as a flux in high temperature glazes, it acts to some extent as an agent in producing semi-matt and matt effects.

Colemanite 2CaO. 3B$_2$O$_3$. 5H$_2$O Eq.Wt.206 Mol.Wt.412
Calcium borate Borocalcite. CaO. 2B$_2$O$_3$. 6H$_2$O Mol.Wt.304
Natural sources of boric oxide, providing powerful primary and secondary fluxes at high and low temperatures. As they are natural fritts, they vary from source to sources and their Mol.Wt. and Eq.Wt. change accordingly.

China clay Al$_2$O$_3$. 2SiO$_2$. 2H$_2$O Mol.Wt.258
Used in glazes to supply both alumina and silica, it produces alumina matts when used in excess and so can also cause crawling of the glaze. It helps to keep the glaze in suspension.

Cornish stone (Average) Mol.Wt.667
0·30 CaO 1·10 APP$_2$O$_3$. 8·10 SiO$_2$
0·36 K$_2$O
0·34 Na$_2$O

Cornish stone K$_2$O Al$_2$O$_3$ 8SiO$_2$ (Theoretical) Mol.Wt.678
An English felspar which requires high temperatures for fusion, melting alone at about 1500°C., it helps to form very hard glazes. There are several varieties with different formulae.

Cryolite Na$_3$ AlF$_6$ Eq.Wt.420 Mol.Wt.210
A source of sodium oxide in an unfritted form, helpful in making alkaline glazes when typical colour responses are being sought.

Felspar (potash) K$_2$O Al$_2$O$_3$ 6SiO$_2$ Mol.Wt.556
Used extensively in glazes and a principal ingredient in high temperature glazes. It melts alone at about 1200–1300°C.

Felspar (soda) Na$_2$O. Al$_2$O$_3$. 6SiO$_2$ Mol.Wt.524
Another form of felspar with a sodium base.

Flint (silica) SiO$_2$ Mol.Wt.60
A source of free silica, infusible at high temperatures, it provides the chief acid substance in glazes. It also exists in the form of quartz.

Magnesium Carbonate MgCO$_3$ Mol.Wt.84
A high temperature flux with good colour responses from cobalt and manganese. It gives a smooth surface to glazes.

Dolomite CaCO$_3$ MgCO$_3$ Mol.Wt.184
Supplies two secondary fluxes, calcium and magnesium in carbonate form, both useful in stoneware glazes.

Nepheline syenite
0·25 K$_2$O. 1·10 Al$_2$O$_3$. 4·65 SiO$_2$ (Average) Mol.Wt.462
0·75 Na$_2$O

A felspar with a lower melting point, due to the higher proportion of sodium and potassium to that of the silica content. The formula varies according to the source of supply, so the Mol.Wt., may need adjustment, as follows:

Nepheline syenite $K_2O. \quad 3Na_2O. \quad 4Al_2O_3. \quad 8SiO_2$ Eq.Wt.389
Mol.Wt.1168

Whiting $CaCO_3$ Mol.Wt.100

The chief source of calcium in glazes and a common flux at high temperatures.

Zinc oxide ZnO Mol.Wt.81

A secondary flux and a matting agent for glazes.

Fritts and fritting

Fritting is the melting together of soluble substances with some insoluble materials to achieve an insoluble glass. Boric oxide, B_2O_3 from borax, soda Na_2O and potash K_2O are alkalis and therefore soluble in water, and as the usual methods of grinding and application by water affect such substances, they have to be rendered insoluble. They are mixed dry, in the same manner as a glass batch and are then melted together. The melted mixture, while still molten is run out of the furnace into tanks of cold water causing it to break up into tiny fragments, which can then be ground into a fine powder.

A further use is made of fritting; in the case of poisonous lead compounds it makes them non-toxic and safer to use, for health regulations demand that the amount of soluble lead in glazes must not exceed 5%. Low Sol glazes have been so treated.

It is also usual to incorporate into the fritt some insoluble substances, so that the sum of the acidic oxides should not be less than the sum of the bases, but not more than three times the sum of the molecular parts of the bases so as to keep the fritt within the range of low fusion.

Nature has of course provided us with natural fritts, such as felspars, but in many cases the natural fritts contain too much alumina and silica, making their use at low temperatures, impracticable.

It is possible, (though not advisable) to use soluble substances in glazes, with precautions, but the disadvantages are many. A mixture of soluble soda and insoluble silica would separate on the surface of the pot, as the watery solution would be absorbed into the porous pot leaving the insoluble substance on the surface. As the soluble materials dissolve in the water medium of the glaze, it makes storage difficult as the water must not be poured off or taken away, but the whole kept in its wet condition. Soluble materials are not easy

Pestle and mortar or a mixing tub

Brush and sieve

Scales, balances and metric weights

Ball mill

Crucible

Fritt Kiln

10. Equipment for raw glazes and ready-made fritts

Vase with celadon glaze on a porcelain body, incised decoration, 12 inches high, reduction fired at 1300 C. No. 19 glaze. By William Ruscoe.

Group of pots in stoneware and porcelain with felspathic glazes and variations of vanadium and iron stains, reduction fired at 1300 C. No.21 glaze. By William Ruscoe, from the collections of G. Adamson, Esq. and F. Ruscoe, Esq.

Group of stonewares. Pot with iron and copper stained glaze, rust painting, oxidised firing at 1300 C. No. 21 glaze. Bowl and small pot with brown-black glaze, iron and ilmenite painting, reduction firing at 1300 C. No. 22 glaze coloured by 10% of iron. By William Ruscoe, from the collection of G. Adamson Esq.

to keep in dry form as they are hygroscopic and take in moisture from the atmosphere. Also some substances such as soda ash are caustic and could injure the skin of the user, unless rubber gloves are worn.

The advantages of using fritts are the lower temperatures at which soluble materials may be incorporated in the glaze, the smoother quality of the glaze as parts of it have been pre-melted, fewer faults such as pin-holing, boiling, volatilization and others characteristic of some raw glazes.

Fritting requires the facilities of a special fritt kiln whereby the ingredients can be melted and a ball mill for the grinding of the cooled fritt to the right particle size. For small quantities a crucible filled with the ingredients and fired at a suitable temperature would serve for the melting process. The crucible would have to be taken out of the furnace while hot and its contents poured into cold water; or it could be allowed to cool in the furnace, after which the contents could be broken out of the crucible and then crushed and ground.

Fritt is composed to give an insoluble substance which will yield the desired fluxes unobtainable from other sources, though not all combinations of flux and acid are insoluble. The addition of lime and/or lead in the fritt helps to make for insolubility. Other oxides, such as alumina, zinc, as well as silica and boric oxide all help to make the fritt insoluble. All the alkalis needed for the glaze would be included in the fritt mixture, especially the soda, otherwise some other source would have to be found. A good insoluble source of potash is felspar, if the silica ratio is not too high. The ratio of alkalis to other bases should be sufficient to make unnecessary any further additions of alkalis to the glaze. It is, however, easy to add other insoluble bases to the batch in order to preserve the balance between the alkalis and other bases of the completed glaze.

Fritts may be, but seldom are, used alone. It is usual to add some of the insoluble substances at the stage of mixing the batch.

Fritting is a comparatively modern innovation and was brought into use partly to make safe the use of lead and to utilise borax and boric acid. Its use divides and classifies glazes into raw glazes and fritted glazes. A third category is found in salt glaze or vapour glaze.

Artist-potters wishing to use fritts may purchase them from suppliers of materials. Some manufacturers publish the formulae of some of their fritts and raw materials which is very helpful. It is easy to understand that manufacturers of glazes will wish to keep the formulae of their products a secret in order to prevent them from being copied by competitors, but if fritts are to be understood and of real value to the individual worker, it is important to have as much knowledge as possible of their make-up. With the information it should be possible to use a fritt in the same manner as felspar or other natural fritt by its molecular parts and weights. There are of course many compositions of fritts for most purposes and the use of them in connection with the colouring oxides needs to be studied by testing; for example to produce the Egyptian turquoise, a high alkaline fritt would be required.

Calculating for a fritt batch is done in the same manner as the calculation for a glaze, except that, as explained, soluble substances are used and followed by the melting, cooling and grinding processes. Where there are no facilities for doing this, it is advisable to purchase fritts ready made, for apart from the equipment required the production of a large number of fritts is a highly specialised job.

In general fritts need not be used at temperatures above 1200°C., as there are plenty of natural fritts, e.g. felspars which operate at this heat. Below this temperature the use of fritts is most advantageous and when the formula of the fritt is known, it follows that the glaze formula can be controlled.

Fritts may be regarded as glazes and may be used as base glazes, to which are added other raw materials. China clay when added assists in glaze suspension and helps the glaze to fit the pot. Free silica in the form of flint can harden and assist against crazing, thus adjusting the fritt to the user's requirements. Fritts may also be mixed and blends of fritt and raw material provide a wide range for experimentation. When formula and molecular weight are known, adjustments can be made to the glaze recipe.

Lead monosilicate PbO. $1 \cdot 0$ SiO_2 Mol. Wt. 283 Temps. 750–960°C.
Lead sesquisilicate PbO. $1 \cdot 5$ SiO_2 Mol. Wt. 313 Temps. 880–1080°C.
Lead bisilicate PbO. $2 \cdot 0$ SiO_2 Mol. Wt. 343 Temps. 900–1100°C.
All safe forms of lead, except lead monosilicate.

Alkaline fritts enable the glaze-maker to produce glazes with alkaline bases for use when their colour responses are sought. A wide range with temps. 900–1100°C.

Borax fritts introduce B_2O_3 into glazes, and fritted with other alkaline ingredients produce leadless glazes. A wide temperature range, from 850–1150°C., and a considerable variety.

Zircon-borax fritt. For opaque glazes at temperatures up to 1150°C.
Zircon-lead fritt. For white opaque glazes, temps. 940–1150°C.

To calculate a fritt as part of a glaze when both formulae are known presents no problem. The fritt is regarded as any other complex compound and the necessary molecular parts are multiplied by the molecular weight of the fritt. If the formula of the fritt is given but not its molecular weight, this can be found by multiplying the quantity of each oxide by its molecular weight and then adding the various results together, in the same manner as the molecular weight of a felspar would be calculated.

1. *Example*. A glaze having the formula, $1 \cdot 0$ PbO. $0 \cdot 2$ Al_2O_3. $2 \cdot 5$ SiO_2 is to be converted into a recipe using

lead bisilicate (fritt) formula	$1 \cdot 0$ PbO	$2 \cdot 0$ SiO_2

the molecular weight of the fritt is 343.

This leaves to be added: $\qquad 0 \cdot 2$ Al_2O_3. $0 \cdot 5$ SiO_2

The same example can be tabulated by the formula to recipe method.

Materials	Mol. Wts.	Mol. Parts.	Parts by Wt.	$1 \cdot 0$ PbO	$0 \cdot 2$ Al_2O_3	$2 \cdot 5$ SiO_2	% Recipe
Lead bisilicate (fritt)	343	$\times$ $1 \cdot 0$	= $343 \cdot 0$	$1 \cdot 0$		$2 \cdot 0$	$85 \cdot 5$
China clay	258	$\times$ $0 \cdot 2$	= $51 \cdot 6$		$0 \cdot 2$	$0 \cdot 4$	$13 \cdot 0$
Flint	60	$\times$ $0 \cdot 1$	= $6 \cdot 0$			$0 \cdot 1$	$1 \cdot 5$
Totals			$400 \cdot 6$	$1 \cdot 0$	$0 \cdot 2$	$2 \cdot 5$	$100 \cdot 0$

Some fritts can be used as suitable glazes with the addition of up to 10 parts of china clay to 100 parts of fritt which helps to keep the wet glaze in suspension, but this addition does alter the formula. The following calculations show this.

2. *Example*: Formula of Wenger alkaline fritt, temp. 900–1100°C.

$0 \cdot 560$ CaO $\quad 0 \cdot 266$ Al_2O_3 $\quad 2 \cdot 400$ SiO_2 $\quad$ Est.Mol.Wt. 255.
$0 \cdot 440$ Na_2O $\qquad\qquad 0 \cdot 363$ B_2O_3

(some authorities place B_2O_3 with SiO_2, others with Al_2O_3).

It is decided to add some china clay to help keep the glaze in suspension, by adding $0 \cdot 1$ Al_2O_3 this brings in $0 \cdot 2$ SiO_2.

The same example can be tabulated by the formula to recipe method:

Materials	Mol. Wts.	Mol. Parts.	Parts. by Wt.	$0 \cdot 560$ CaO	$0 \cdot 440$ Na_2O	$0 \cdot 366$ Al_2O_3	$2 \cdot 600$ SiO_2	$0 \cdot 363$ B_2O_3	% Recipe
Alkaline fritt.	255	$\times$ $1 \cdot 0$	= 255	$0 \cdot 560$	$0 \cdot 440$	$0 \cdot 266$	$2 \cdot 400$	$0 \cdot 363$	91
China clay	258	$\times$ $0 \cdot 1$	= $25 \cdot 8$			$0 \cdot 100$	$0 \cdot 200$		9
Totals			$280 \cdot 8$	$0 \cdot 560$	$0 \cdot 440$	$0 \cdot 366$	$2 \cdot 600$	$0 \cdot 363$	100

Chapter VI

Formulating new glazes

There are a number of important factors to be considered in the process of firing. The potter must decide on a specific clay or body, and work out the technique of biscuit and maturing temperatures, as well as determining the type of kiln to be used and whether the wares are to be fired in an oxidising or a reducing atmosphere.

A glance at the limiting formulae of the alumina-silica ratios will assist in determining the appropriate temperature to use in accordance with the acid/amphoteric proportions present and limiting formulae for bases will again help in the selection of suitable bases for the chosen temperature.

Whether the glaze is to be entirely raw or whether fritts will be used are further considerations.

In the process of understanding the make-up of glazes and particularly when evolving new ones, it is obvious that high and low limits of the oxides occur. Certain limits of silica are understandable at the various temperatures and glazes have always more than one ratio of silica to that of the bases. The ratio of alumina is usually 1/10th to 1/6th, to that of the acid substances, but the bases are more numerous and have different fluxing powers. It is in this area that consideration must be given to the selection and availability of bases, particularly when insoluble sources are required.

Limiting formulae can only indicate in the broadest way a coverage of the many variables of glaze composition. The limits indicated by the chart and the table can be most helpful as a guide to which basic oxide to use and to how much, according to the type and nature of the glaze.

Unless otherwise stated, it should be remembered that any rules or laws formulated about making glazes are those which apply to making a clear colourless glass and not one which may be matt, cloudy, opaque, or in any way different to the conception of what is a good glass. The chemist may be in pursuit of a glass which is technically perfect and one which is to be reproduced in large quantities and on an economical basis. The artist-potter may wish to take advantage of the odd effect of mattness, texture, broken colour, or even of cracks and crazes, as did the Chinese.

Matt glazes may be regarded as unbalanced glazes, and the rules are broken in some way to achieve a new effect. Overloading of the glaze with one or more substances is an example of this.

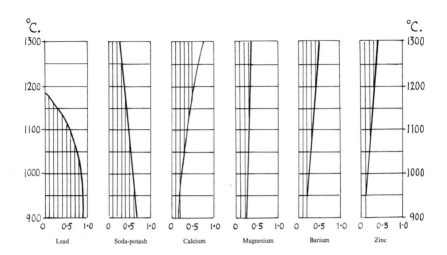

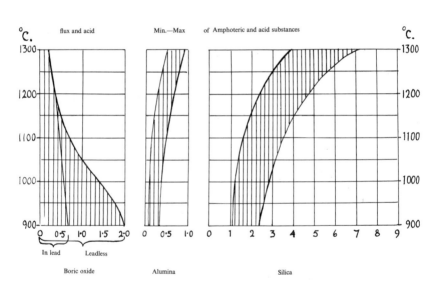

11. Guide to qualities of basic fluxes used in glazes

At high or very low temperatures it is reasonably easy to compound glazes, starting with the felspars for the high temperatures and adding single oxide basic fluxes, such as calcium, barium or magnesium to adjust the high ratio of the silica content of the felspar.

At low temperatures the use of lead will suggest itself as a base needing silica to make it into a bisilicate and a little clay to provide the amphoteric. It is in the middle range of temperatures, about 1150°C. to 1250°C., that glazes become more complex mixtures, especially if fritting is to be avoided.

The age-old methods of mixing by measure or weight the unknown materials, and firing them to see what would happen could take a long time. Adjustments following firing trials would also be time consuming and extend over long periods. Observation, followed by trial and error, would in time establish certain results, but there would be some mystery surrounding the whole operation.

In using molecular formulae to adjust the glass-forming materials, we are taking a shorter cut and a much more practical one, but all new materials and compositions have to be tried, adjusted and proved in performance. In this way glaze-making can be considered to be experimental, but making use of the information supplied by research workers and the published formulae of the various minerals, oxides and substances offered by the suppliers controls the area of experimentation.

The limiting formulae of glazes are, however, generalisations and there are many exceptions, but they do serve as a guide and provide the necessary clues. Knowledge and experience all play their part in using the various substances and writing down a formula within the limits of the known field.

Devising a glaze formula, by selection from limiting formulae

A stoneware glaze to fire at 1300°C., is required. From the limiting formulae it will be seen that the ratios of alumina and silica for this temperature are $0 \cdot 5$–$0 \cdot 9$ Al_2O_3 and $4 \cdot 0$–$7 \cdot 2$ SiO_2 giving a very wide range of possible figures. Three common bases are chosen (giving consideration to possible colour responses) with maximum limits of $0 \cdot 275$ K_2O. $0 \cdot 750$ Al_2O_3. $0 \cdot 500$ BaO. Selecting some low limits and keeping the bases within unity a formula is written as follows:

$$\left.\begin{array}{l} 0 \cdot 25\ K_2O \\ 0 \cdot 50\ CaO \\ 0 \cdot 25\ BaO \end{array}\right\} \quad 0 \cdot 60\ Al_2O_3 \quad 4 \cdot 50\ SiO_2$$

12. Group of stoneware pots with brown-
black and grey glazes, and iron and
cobalt decoration; reduction firing at
1300°C. By William Ruscoe, from
the collection of F. Ruscoe

The same example can be tabulated and worked into a recipe by the formula to recipe method.

Materials	Mol. Wts.	Mol. Parts	Parts by Wt.	0·25 K$_2$O	0·50 CaO	0·25 BaO	0·60 Al$_2$O$_3$	4·50 SiO$_2$	% Recipe
Potash felspar	556 ×	0·25 =	139·0	0·25			0·25	1·50	30·0
Whiting	100 ×	0·50 =	50·0		0·50				10·5
Barium carbonate	197 ×	0·25 =	49·2			0·25			10·0
China clay	258 ×	0·35 =	90·3				0·35	0·70	19·5
Flint	60 ×	2·30 =	138·0					2·30	30·0
Totals			466·5	0·25	0·50	0·25	0·60	4·50	100·0

Building a glaze around colemanite, to fire at about 1200°C.

Another method of devising a glaze is to select a glass forming mineral and to add other requirements through a molecular formula and afterwards working it through to a recipe. In this case colemanite is selected with a formula of 2CaO. 3B$_2$O$_3$. 5H$_2$O Mol.Wt.412 Eq.Wt.206. It will be seen that the other bases, alumina and silica are required and that only a small amount of colemanite may be used on account of its high B$_2$O$_3$. Introducing 0·1 part of colemanite would yield 0·15 B$_2$O$_3$ and 0·1 of CaO; another 0·45 of CaO (from whiting) would build the CaO to its limit. Magnesium might be brought in up to 0·3 parts and the remainder of the bases made up to unity by using 0·15 of K$_2$O, a felspar giving some alumina and silica, which can be further increased by china clay and flint. If a matt glaze is sought, a fairly high amount of 0·4 Al$_2$O$_3$ and a low limit of 2·5 SiO$_2$ would set the formula as follows.

$$0.55 \text{ CaO} \quad 0.40 \text{ Al}_2\text{O}_3$$
$$0.30 \text{ MgO} \quad 0.15 \text{ B}_2\text{O}_3 \quad 2.50 \text{ SiO}_2$$
$$0.15 \text{ K}_2\text{O}$$

Tabulating the colemanite first and using its Eq.Wt.206 because its formula contains 2 molecules of CaO, so we divide the formula by 2 to obtain 1·0 molecule of CaO and 1·5 molecules of B$_2$O$_3$. Only 0·1 molecular parts of colemanite is needed to give 0·1 CaO and 0·15 molecules of B$_2$O$_3$ which is the amount of B$_2$O$_3$ required. The H$_2$O is disregarded.

Materials	Mol. Wts.	Mol. Parts	Parts by Wt.	0·55 CaO	0·30 MgO	0·15 K_2O	0·40 Al_2O_3	0·15 B_2O_3	2·50 SiO_2	% Recipe
Colemanite	206 × 0·10 = 20·6 (Eq. Wt.)			0·10				0·15		7
Magnesium carbonate	84 × 0·30 = 25·2				0·30					8
Whiting	100 × 0·45 = 45·0			0·45						15
Potash felspar	556 × 0·15 = 83·4					0·15	0·15		0·90	27
China clay	258 × 0·25 = 64·5						0·25		0·50	21
Flint	60 × 1·10 = 66·0								1·10	22
Totals			304·7	0·55	0·30	0·15	0·40	0·15	2·50	100

Building a glaze, using dolomite and felspar to fire at 1300°C.

Formula of dolomite $CaCO_3$ $MgCO_3$ Mol.Wt.184.

Dolomite has equal molecular parts of CaO and MgO; the CO_2 can be ignored as it is burnt off, but it is accounted for in the Mol.Wt. of the dolomite.

Acting on this, the bases for the glaze could be made up within the maximum limits, obtaining the alumina and silica ratios from felspar, china clay and flint for the appropriate temperature.

The formula could be written:

From dolomite $\begin{cases} 0·345 \text{ CaO} \\ 0·345 \text{ MgO} \end{cases}$

$$0·5 \text{ } Al_2O_3 \quad 4·0 \text{ } SiO_2$$

From felspar   0·250 K_2O

Additional whiting   0·060 CaO

To give unity   1·000

Materials	Mol. Wts.	Mol. Parts	Parts by Wt.	0·405 CaO	0·345 MgO	0·250 K_2O	0·50 Al_2O_3	4·0 SiO_2	% Recipe
Dolomite	184 × 0·345 = 83·48			0·345	0·345				20·0
Whiting	100 × 0·060 = 6·00			0·060					1·5
Potash felspar	556 × 0·250 = 139·00					0·250	0·25	1·5	34·0
China clay	258 × 0·250 = 64·50						0·25	0·5	15·5
Flint	60 × 2·000 = 120·00							2·0	29·0
Totals			412·98	0·405	0·345	0·250	0·50	4·0	100·0

Building a glaze using nepheline syenite, to fire at 1200°C.

Formula of nepheline syenite;

$$0.25 \ K_2O \qquad 1.10 \ Al_2O_3 \qquad 4.65 \ SiO_2$$
$$0.75 \ Na_2O_3$$

By using 0.5 molecular parts of nepheline syenite and dividing its formula by 2 we have:

$0.125 \ K_2O$	$0.550 \ Al_2O_3$	$2.325 \ SiO_2$
$0.375 \ Na_2O$		

adding 0.5 whiting $\quad 0.500 \ CaO$

adding 0.15 china clay $\qquad\qquad 0.150 \ Al_2O_3 \qquad 0.300 \ SiO_2$

gives the formula $\quad 1.000 \qquad\qquad 0.700 \qquad\qquad 2.625$

Materials	Mol. Wts.	Mol. Parts	Parts by Wt.	0.125 K_2O	0.375 Na_2O	0.500 CaO	0.700 Al_2O_3	2.625 SiO_2	% Recipe
Nepheline syenite	462 ×	0.5 =	231.0	0.125	0.375		0.550	2.325	72.2
Whiting	100 ×	0.5 =	50.0			0.500			15.6
China clay	258 ×	0.15 =	38.7				0.150	0.300	12.2
Totals			319.7	0.125	0.375	0.500	0.700	2.625	100.0

This gives a matt glaze, due to the low silica content and high alumina. More silica and a higher temperature would give gloss.

Matt glazes

These may be produced in various ways, but are caused by the formation of countless microscopic crystals in the glaze, brought about by adjustments to the composition of the glaze which will cause devitrification to take place when conditions of cooling are suitable. They can be regarded as unbalanced glazes, for a perfect glass would have a smooth shiny surface, whereas a matt glaze has a dull texture. They may also be regarded as crystalline glazes although the crystals are not large. When glazes are not completely melted they are often matt in texture, only to become bright and smooth when refired to a maturing temperature. The qualities of mattness and opacity are related, due to the undissolved particles which prevent the glaze from becoming amorphous thus obstructing the passage of light.

Matt effects can be produced by an increase in the alumina content or by an increase of silica both of which could cause devitrification, but a variety of matts are due to an excess of some other agent.

Alumina matt is produced when alumina exceeds the usual limits, but this often only results in a rough surface.

13. Pebble shaped pot in stoneware, chromium and iron coloured textures with matt glaze; reduction firing at 1300°C. The tall pot has manganese coloured texture, cream matt glaze; oxidised firing at 1200°C. By William Ruscoe

Zinc matts usually have a narrow fusion range and certain colours turn brown, but blues and browns develop in intensity.

Lime matts show true colours and are usually used when the wares are to be decorated by painting under the glaze.

Barium matt has a pleasant texture which may be achieved by the use of celsian, a barium felspar or by barium carbonate.

The disadvantages of matt glazes are that they are not so easy to wash clean and are likely to stain. When sculptural forms need to be glazed these surfaces are very attractive.

Colours react differently according to the nature of the bases used.

Blending and testing of glazes, varying one component, silica

Testing of glazes can be time consuming. Accurate and systematic blending can save much time when working through a set of variations of a particular component. Instead of mixing many glazes, only the end members of the set need to be tested. The dry materials of these are weighed out accurately from the percentage recipes and the same amount of water is added to each. After mixing, the specific gravity of each may be checked by separately weighing an equal volume of each. Should the weight of the glazes differ a little more water can be added to adjust the difference. The blending can then be done in the wet state, using a graduated measure for the various proportions of the two glazes. All the blended tests are then fired at the same temperature as well as the tests of the end members. After firing, the results can be assessed for crazing, brilliancy, colour or whatever is being sought.

Two glazes to be tested, having different ratios of silica:

A 0.6 PbO
   0.3 CaO 0.2 Al$_2$O$_3$ 1.6 SiO$_2$
   0.1 K$_2$O

B 0.6 PbO
   0.3 CaO 0.2 Al$_2$O$_3$ 2.0 SiO$_2$
   0.1 K$_2$O

Proportions by measurement in volume of equal specific gravity:

Glaze A	100	87	75	62	50	38	25	13	0
Glaze B	0	13	25	38	50	62	75	87	100
Silica ratios	1·6	1·65	1·7	1·75	1·8	1·85	1·9	1·95	2·0

Blending a glaze with two variables of B$_2$O$_3$ and Al$_2$O$_3$

In this case a matt glaze is sought. Two formulae are worked into recipes and mixed with equal volumes of water and measured in five differing proportions of equal specific gravity.

A 0.2 K$_2$O
  0.1 MgO 0.35 B$_2$O$_3$ 2.8 SiO$_2$
  0.7 CaO 0.25 Al$_2$O$_3$

B 0.2 K$_2$O
  0.1 MgO 0.15 B$_2$O$_3$ 2.8 SiO$_2$
  0.7 CaO 0.45 Al$_2$O$_3$

Fired at 1080°C. on a white earthenware body, the results were as follows:

A	100	75	50	25	0
B	0	25	50	75	100

Bright	Semi-matt	Matt	Dry matt	Rough matt

The 50/50 mixture formula

0.2 K$_2$O
            0.25 B$_2$O$_3$
0.1 MgO 2.8 SiO$_2$
            0.35 Al$_2$O$_3$
0.7 CaO

Varying three components: in this case the bases are changed

Glaze formulae for stoneware to fire at about 1280°C.

A $\begin{array}{l} 0\cdot3\ K_2O \\ 0\cdot7\ CaO \end{array}$ $0\cdot6\ Al_2O_3$. $3\cdot6\ SiO_2$

B $\begin{array}{l} 0\cdot3\ K_2O \\ 0\cdot4\ CaO \\ 0\cdot3\ BaO \end{array}$ $0\cdot6\ Al_2O_3$. $3\cdot6\ SiO_2$

C $\begin{array}{l} 0\cdot3\ K_2O \\ 0\cdot4\ CaO \\ 0\cdot3\ MgO \end{array}$ $0\cdot6\ Al_2O_3$. $3\cdot6\ SiO_2$

The formulae are brought to recipe form and when the materials are mixed with water to the same specific gravity, they are then blended by volume to give the variables. To achieve this, a three component diagram is drawn, based on an equal-sided triangle ABC. Each point in the triangle represents the sum of the three compositions in the corners. The proportion of any two substances can be found on opposite sides of the triangle by drawing parallel lines.

The proportions of any mixture of three substances can be placed where the lines join, thus E represents 50% C, 25% A and 25% B. Point D represents 70% A and 30% C.

14 A diagram to find the blending variables of three components in a glaze

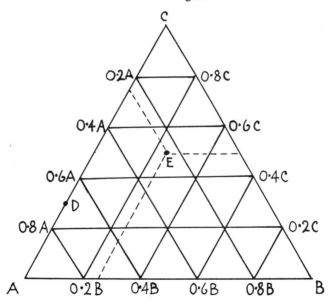

Blending variables of alumina and silica; the bases being at unity

A	RO	$0\cdot3$ Al_2O_3.	$4\cdot0$ SiO_2	10	20	30	40	25
B	RO	$0\cdot3$ Al_2O_3.	$5\cdot0$ SiO_2	40	10	20	30	25
C	RO	$0\cdot5$ Al_2O_3.	$4\cdot0$ SiO_2	30	40	10	20	25
D	RO	$0\cdot5$ Al_2O_3.	$5\cdot0$ SiO_2	20	30	40	10	25

Each glaze can be tested separately as well as through the above simple permutations. Many others are possible, giving further blends. Each of the following combinations could represent two of the glazes, which again could be mixed, tested and assessed, working through to a final formula of the best one.

A   B   C   D   This line represents 100% of each.
     A–B   A–C   A–D   Each of the double mixtures could represent,
            B–C   B–D   50/50% or 75/25%, or 25/75% and many
                   C–D   others.

Over-blending can lead to muddy mixtures of grey and brown when colour is concerned. It is better to test for colour responses in simple combinations or mixtures.

Chapter VII

Colour in glazes

Many artist-potters, teachers, students and others elect to buy prepared coloured glazes or basic glazes to which are added colouring oxides. This is perhaps the best way to go about getting results when knowledge is slight.

Manufacturers do not usually disclose the recipes or composition of their glazes and this gives a somewhat false and unsatisfactory situation, as the user of the glaze may not know anything about its nature. Many potters will wish to advance and to acquire more knowledge so as to be able to produce something which is personal, creative and under control. In the case of teachers and students, it is also more educative.

It will be seen that coloured glazes may be produced in several ways; from the colour in the clay, or colour applied to the clay or biscuit and therefore underneath the glaze, to colour added to the colourless glaze and to colour applied on top of the glaze before or after its firing. The latter application, which includes enamels and pastes to produce lustre, must receive a further firing to enable it to adhere or sink into the glaze.

The most usual method is to add varying amounts of colouring oxides to the glaze before it is applied to the pot. This may be done by adding dry parts by weight of colour, to dry parts by weight of glaze. Thus: 100 parts of glaze, which could be in grams, ounces or pounds, etc., could have 1 or more parts of colouring matter added to it, using dry weight. Although not actual percentages, the smaller parts are more easily calculated by this method.

The ceramic-artist cannot rely on any simple rule, nor see any tangible results, until the emergence from the kiln of the calculated tests, for the colours of the oxides are dissimilar before and after firing. Fine grinding assists the oxides to be assimilated into the glaze and water-ground colours are usually better in this respect than those which are dry-ground.

When making tests and assuming that the base glaze has been determined, it is best to test each oxide singly and in varying proportions, according to the minimum and maximum amounts of oxide that the glaze will contain. As the oxides have various chromatic values and are very much affected by the heat treatment, some become fugitive and burn away while others such as cobalt seem to develop in intensity, withstanding all temperatures.

Bowl in porcelain with a felspathic glaze and brush strokes in copper. No. 24 glaze. The jar is in stoneware and has a white opaque glaze superimposed over the copper stained glaze. Both had light reduction firing at 1300 C. By William Ruscoe.

Jar with brown-black glaze on a porcelain body, incised decoration, 12 inches high, reduction fired at 1300 C. No. 19 glaze. By William Ruscoe.

Group of earthenwares. Bowl, vase and jar with alkaline glazes, copper colouring, incised decoration through a white slip on a brown body, oxidised
firing at 1080 C. No. 3 glaze. By William Ruscoe.

Group of pots in stoneware with felspathic glazes and colourings from rutile,
cobalt, iron and manganese. On the left the pot is glazed with No. 23 glaze.
The carved texture of the blue pot by Mrs. L. Lord, retains the matt glaze
No. 20 thickly. The wave shaped bowl was salt-glazed by Bob and Jo Monro
of New Zealand. The bird decoration is scratched through a slip of manganese. Temperatures range from 1200 C. to 1300 C. and oxidising as well as
reduction firings were used.

15. Stoneware pot with grey-green glaze and painted iron decoration, 2ft. 6in. high, reduction firing at 1300°C. By William Ruscoe

The amount of colouring matter that a glaze will take before it becomes over saturated also varies with the oxide. Too much metallic oxide may cause it to float about on the surface of the glaze, but some advantage may be taken of this to produce metallic effects. However, the glaze is really being changed by an overdose of metal.

The artist with an eye to the colour responses of the various minerals must also bear in mind the facts about the glass forming substances, for although they may be colourless in themselves they do affect the colouring oxides, sometimes in a most remarkable way. The experimenter must expect disappointments as well as successes, but at least knowledge will be acquired and experience of the materials will enable results to be achieved.

The colouring oxides

It will have been noticed that silica plays a dominant role in the field of ceramics. Iron also takes an important part, well established by the fact of its existence in most earths and rocks. In clays, only the kaolins are comparatively free from its contaminating influence. The early potters using the brown earths were unable to get rid of it, but they never ceased in their efforts to make white pottery.

A white engobe or slip of light sand and the opaque glaze of the Near East are evidence of the efforts to cover the dark clays of the Nile and the Euphrates areas. The Chinese, with their white porcelain, were probably the first to produce a white ceramic body over which a transparent glaze could be put, giving a totally white appearance throughout. In present day technology the iron particles can be extracted by magnetic attraction and we have white bodies of various kinds suitable for many purposes.

The artist-potter wishing to use the iron bearing clays, fireclay and red clay, should remember that iron may affect the colour of a glaze on contact, as well as at the fusion point of body and glaze.

Oxygen is also a prevalent element and most of the metals of the earth's crust enter into combination with it to give us oxides. The oxides are chiefly used for ceramic colours, as well as some carbonates.

Antimony oxide Sb_2O_3. Gives weak whites. 10–20%

Antimoniate of lead $Pb_3(SbO_4)_2$. In lead glazes it gives Naples yellow at temperatures up to 1050°C. 5–10%

Chromium oxide Cr_2O_3. This produces an opaque green colouration which is rather changeable. Yellow and red in some lead-type glazes, and pink when in combination with tin. 1–3%

Cobalt carbonate $CoCO_3$. Cobalt oxide. Co_3O_4. Most powerful of pigments, giving blues. In the presence of magnesium, the colour becomes purple. Does not burn away. 0·5–2%

Copper carbonate $CuCO_3$. Copper oxide. CuO. In lead glazes the oxide yields grass-greens, in alkaline glazes the carbonate gives turquoise and blues. When reduced in a suitable glaze copper-reds will ensue. Fluxing. 1–5%

Ilmenite (ferrous titanate) $FeO.TiO_2$. Gives an iron colouration and areas of spots and specks. 1–7%

Iron compounds Are used in many forms: ferric oxide Fe_2O_3, ferrous oxide FeO, ferroso-ferric oxide Fe_3O_4, and others. A wide range of colours are produced from iron, according to the nature of the glaze used and the method of firing. When oxidation firing takes place, warm creams, yellows, red-browns and blacks emerge. In reduction firings, the warm colours become cool and celadon greens and blues are possible. 1–10%

Iron chromate Fe_2O_3. Cr_2O_3. Produces grey. 1–3%

Manganese carbonate $MnCO_3$. Manganese oxide. MnO_2. Gives brown in lead glazes and purple in alkaline glazes. Mixed with cobalt a violet colour will develop. Fluxing. 2–10%

Nickel oxide NiO. Colours from nickel tend to be dull and uncertain. Usually produces greys. 1–3%

Potassium bichromate $K_2Cr_2O_7$. Used to produce orange and red in lead glazes. 900°C. Soluble, used as fritt. 1–10%

Rutile TiO_2. A colourant which does not dissolve, giving brown specks and streaks. Titanium bearing iron. 2–10%

Titanium Oxide TiO_2. Gives whites and creams. 5–10%

Tin oxide SnO_2. The much used opacifier from ancient times. Gives soft snowy whites, semi-opaque at 5%, opaque at 10%

Uranium oxide U_3O_8. (Depleted) used to give flame-coloured orange to red in soft lead glazes. 2–7%

Vanadium pentoxide V_2O_5. Depending on the nature of the glaze, temperature and firing conditions, a variety of colours can be obtained. Yellow with tin, blue-grey to black if reduced. 5–10%

Zirconium oxide ZrO_2. and compounds give white opacity. It is refractory but extra amounts are required. Up to 15%

Cadmium and selenium are used to produce orange and red glazes at low temperatures, 980–1080°C. The colours are fugitive if over-fired and it is usual to buy prepared glazes.

Other ways of colouring glazes are to purchase ready-mixed glaze stains, which are mixtures of oxides, carbonates, etc., expertly put together for this service. These can be added as percentages or parts to the glaze, but it should always be remembered that the final outcome, as regards colour, will depend on the nature of the colour-less bases of the glaze, as well as on the degree of opacity and mattness.

Oxidation and reduction

Fuels such as wood, coal, oil and gas all burn upon ignition in air, producing heat. Substances burn in air simply because air contains oxygen and combustion in air is a process of oxidation in which heat and light are liberated. If insufficient oxygen is present at the firing, then carbon monoxide is produced and smoke will result from incomplete combustion. When a plentiful supply of oxygen is present the burning is bright and the atmosphere in the kiln is oxidising. If there is insufficient oxygen a reducing atmosphere prevails. At the high temperatures needed to fire ceramics, the carbon and carbon monoxide will remove oxygen from clay, glaze, and colours and although certain oxides are unaffected the colours of the metallic oxides become greatly affected.

Reduction is more readily achieved in kilns which burn wood, coal, oil and gas, than it is with electrical furnaces where radiant heat from the elements does the baking. In fact reduction shortens the life of the electrical elements of the kiln. It may, however, be achieved but a reduction firing should be followed by many normal oxidising firings. No doubt primitive and inefficient kilns would be smoky at times, but the ancient potters protected their wares from the flames and smoke by means of baffles and saggers which were perforated to allow reduction to take place. A strongly reducing atmosphere will cause only slight reduction of the contents of a sagger. This is important when the potter wishes to fire wares which need varying degrees of reduction in the same kiln.

Reducing atmospheres are achieved by a partial cutting down of the air supply, but not by complete exclusion, otherwise combustion will fail. Burning smoke-producing substances in the chamber sometimes helps, but much depends on the type of kiln being used.

Leadless colourless glazes are not greatly affected by reduction, but lead glazes and those containing zinc should not be reduced. Many colouring oxides do react to a smoky atmosphere. Iron oxides give the cool sea-greens, olive-greens and blues, known as celadons, when reduced. If oxidised these would be warm and creamy in colour. The most spectacular of changes are the copper-reds, for slight reduction changes the usual greens from copper oxides to reds which can vary from blood-red to purple-red. These colours are uncertain in result, much depending on the amount of reduction and the amount of colloidal copper produced within the glaze.

Local reduction, achieved by introducing silicon carbide into the

The bonfire. Pots are open fired over a wood fire to a biscuit. Only low temperatures are possible.

The enclosed fire. Pots are top loaded and fired to a biscuit. Only low temperatures are possible. Oxidation and reduction are both possible.

The enclosed fire. Pots are guarded from the flame and can be biscuit-fired or glaze fired in the down-draught. Oxidation and reduction are both possible.

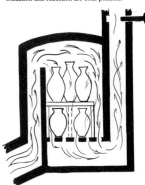

The enclosed fire. Pots are side loaded and over an open flame with a down-draught can be biscuit-fired or glaze fired. Oxidation and reduction are both possible.

The enclosed fire. Pots are guarded from the flame and are side loaded and can be biscuit fired and glaze fired, in the updraught of heat. Oxidation and reduction are both possible

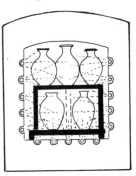

The electric kiln for oxidation.

16. Developments and principles of firing

glaze, can also bring about interesting results, enabling the firing to be done in an electric furnace.

Kilns and firing

In practice, reduction firing depends very much on the kiln, its system of air intake, the fuel involved and the timing of the period of reduction during the firing. For high temperature glazes, no reduction is needed before about 950°C., this may be followed by alternating periods of reduction and oxidation until the end of the firing.

Alternatively, reduction may start at 950°C., and continue up to the final temperature, finishing in either case with oxidation. It is important to keep the temperature steadily rising and a watch should be kept on this and on the amount of smoke being emitted from the chimney.

The surface qualities of glazes are often favourably affected by reduction; for example, the colour of porcelain is improved, becoming whiter and less creamy. Protection from the flames is often needed in open furnaces in order to keep the atmosphere still, which results in uniform colour on the insides of pots.

Chapter VIII

The application of glaze to the pottery

The raw materials for glazing can be bought ready ground and of the correct particle size. If further grinding is required then a ball-mill is used. After calculating and weighing, all that is necessary is to add water to the correct consistency and to pass the whole through a 120 mesh sieve. Sieves are in many grades, 60, 80, 100, 120 or 200 meshes per inch; for clay slip, glaze and colour and it is important to pass all the particles through the mesh so that none of the ingredients are sieved out.

There are mainly four methods of application; dipping or immersion, pouring and swilling, spraying and painting. The quickest and the most effective way is to dip the ware into enough liquid glaze to enable the whole to be totally immersed, after which the article is withdrawn and allowed to drip and dry as the water is sucked into the porous pot leaving an even thickness of glaze on the surface. In order to do this effectively, three things need to be considered; the thickness or density of the glaze liquid, the porosity of the biscuit and the length of time it is immersed. The latter is usually just a brief second or two.

When there is only a small amount of glaze liquid and the pot is too large to dip, then pouring and swilling will enable the glazer to cover the pot with only a small amount of glaze liquid. First the pot should be glazed inside by pouring a little of the liquid inside it and swilling it around before pouring out the remainder. Then the outside of the pot can be dealt with by pouring a waterfall of glaze over the pot. A turntable with a bowl, across which is placed two triangular strips of wood greatly assists this. The turntable can keep the pot moving under a stationary waterfall. The duration of this process again depends on the same conditions; thickness of glaze, porosity of the biscuit and the time of pouring, which can be repeated in order to build up the thickness of the glaze coating, when necessary.

Spraying requires some mechanical aid, such as an air-compressor and gun, although for just a small pot a vapour spraying hand or mouth apparatus can be used. Spraying glaze and colour, however, requires a spraying booth and a fan extractor, particularly if the glaze contains poisonous contents. It is also rather wasteful unless the waste can be collected, but it enables the glazer to control the application of the glaze, building up the coating to the required strength.

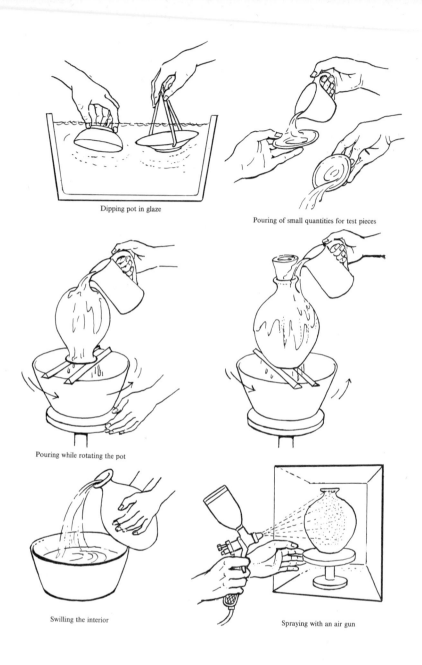

Dipping pot in glaze

Pouring of small quantities for test pieces

Pouring while rotating the pot

Swilling the interior

Spraying with an air gun

17. Application of glazes

Direct painting on the unfired glaze

Wax-resist with colour brushed over

Raised outline to confine the glaze

Different coloured glazes filled in

Dark glaze

Superimposed with lighter glaze

Fused together

18. Decorative methods

Painting, is perhaps the most difficult and least used method of all, except for touching up or for small areas, as a water-based glaze is not easy to apply and an even coating is most difficult to achieve. When dipping, spraying and other methods are impractical, then the glaze can be made into a thixotropic condition by the addition of gelatine, about 1oz to 1 pint of glaze, or 2 to 5%. The dissolved gelatine should be added to a very thick glaze slip and the warm solution allowed to cool into a blancmange-like consistency and then used as paint. Often five or six coats will be needed to build up a uniformly thick coating of glaze. It is advisable to mix and use as required, as the jelly does not keep well.

This method is used for very large pieces, when spraying is difficult and particularly in the case of opaque coloured glaze where flatness of colour is required. It is useful for painting glaze on to the unfired clay and for once-fired wares, especially when cut-glaze decoration is attempted, as the glaze does not flake off when cut into. The Chinese potters of Tze chow may have used a similar technique in their cut-glaze decorations and only single-fired them, as the cutting tool marks can be clearly seen where they go through the layer of glaze and into the clay, leaving bare much of the body of the pot.

Decoration and techniques
A pot which has well balanced form, good proportions and an appropriate glaze will need no further decoration. The finest examples in museums and private collections show this. Nevertheless man has always decorated the artifacts he makes in various ways and nature often shows the way with patterns and textures.

On plain, simple forms the glaze will find ways of achieving interest by running thickly or thinly according to the nature of the glaze and the temperature it receives. Colour and texture will break on rims and shoulders, it will pool thickly in hollows and in various ways the untreated glaze will suffice.

Painting under the glaze
With oxides or prepared underglaze colours, the glaze should be transparent so that the painted decoration can show through. The colours need a little medium, gum and water or turpentine and fat oil, to facilitate the painting and to fix them on to the ware prior to firing. When an oily medium is used, this should be fired out at about 600°C., in a separate firing so that the water glaze will take on to the painted surface. A white body is usual if true

19. Group of pots, brown-black glaze
with rust decoration; reduction firing
at 1300°C. The cream glazed pot has
wax resist decoration washed over
with iron; oxidised firing at 1200°C.
By William Ruscoe

colours are required and the range of colours is restricted according to temperature; yellows and reds tend to burn away above 1100°C., and in the stoneware and porcelain range the palette is limited to blues, greys and browns. Some matt glazes, if not too opaque, permit the colours to show through.

In-glaze painting

This relies on an opaque or matt glaze. The painting is executed on-to the unfired glaze, or the glaze may be partly fused at a previous firing in order to fix the glaze and to make it easier to paint over. When the painting is fused on at the glaze firing, it sinks into the glaze surface and becomes part of the glaze layer. A little of the glaze being used can be added to oxides to make them smooth and glossy, but if prepared colours are used this is not necessary. Examples at low temperatures are the tin enamelled or Delft wares, both monochrome in cobalt blue or polychrome in yellow, green, purple and brown.

At high temperatures, the oriental stonewares painted with brown and black pigments on matt glazes are excellent examples. The brushwork is sharp and crisp, but when the same iron pigments are painted on to shiny glazes the brushwork tends to diffuse and disperse into the glaze like showers of fireworks. The underlying principle being as follows: a matt glaze for hard-edged brushwork and a softer shiny glaze for soft blurry edges. The aesthetic is whatever is pleasing to sight and touch, but it is recommended that the brushwork of the Eastern potters should be studied in appreciation of this style of decoration.

On-glaze or enamel painting

This is a somewhat different process, as it is essentially an applied form of decoration on top of the glaze and only fixed to it by fusion at a lower temperature. Enamels are used with a turpentine and oil medium and a full range of colour is possible, as well as gold, silver and the oxidised lustres. The firing temperature for enamels is around 750–850°C.

Glaze used on raised or sunk carved surfaces

The celadon glazes of the Chinese, Koreans and Japanese are all excellent examples of this treatment. The coloured glaze becomes thicker and deeper in colour in the depths of the carving and lighter on the heights and ridges. Thus the subtle colour graduations are

Painted with wax-resist

Glaze dipped or brushed over

Trailed with coloured glazes for a random effect when the ware is fired

Cut glaze on clay

Splashed with colouring oxides

20. Decorative methods

enhanced by the carving. Finely etched lines and heavy carving all respond to this technique for which translucent glazes are most suitable. The decoration consists of cutting the surface of the pot and the glaze does the rest.

Another method, which consists of a raised line to separate different coloured glazes is mainly suitable for tiles. The glazes can be painted in the hollows between the ridges and this permits patterns of colour to be arranged. Spanish tiles are often treated in this manner, but it cannot be used much on vertical or rounded surfaces due to the flow of the glazes.

Cut and incised glaze

This technique, perfected by the Chinese in the Sung Dynasty, again depends on glazes which do not run together excessively. It can be best executed as a once-for-all firing technique, with still glazes at stoneware temperatures. The brown to black glaze was applied to the dry clay pot, possibly with a gummy adhesive and the decoration was cut through the glaze and often into the clay, leaving the parts from where the glaze had been removed quite bare. The pot could then receive its single firing of both clay and glaze. The risk of the pot exploding in the first and only firing must be taken, and there is also the possibility of glaze flaking off during the cutting unless gum or gelatine is added.

Wax masking

A method of reserving an area or ground is to paint on liquid wax which resists the glaze slip when dipped, sprayed or poured. It can also be used on top of the glaze to mask out part or parts when a second glaze is superimposed and also on the glaze or body before extra pigment is brushed on. It is used in many ways when glaze and colour are not required, such as on the feet or rims of pots. Ordinary candle wax must be heated to make it usable, but wax emulsions are easy to use and they can be painted directly on to the surface to be reserved.

Superimposed or double glazes

These often yield interesting results, particularly when a soft fusible glaze is placed over a hard and still glaze, or the two are reversed. The glazes interact, and boiling during fusion produces flecked and spotted effects as well as diffusion of the two glazes. The glazes should be opposites in some way, matt against shiny, white on colour and so on.

70

Spattering and splashing

When done with glazes or oxides, similar effects to the above are produced, relying on fortuitous results rather than controlled effects.

Lustre glaze and painting

Iridescent colour depends on an extremely thin film of metal being deposited on the surface of the glaze. Persian, Arabian, Hispano-Moresque and Italian painters all developed this technique, but it is seldom now produced. The glazes in the 1000–1100°C. range should not be too high in lead on account of blackening and a little tin is helpful. For lustre glazes or all-over effects, metallic salts and carbonates are added to the glaze and oxidised, but reduction must take place during the cooling period. Lustre painting is done on the previously fired glaze and the metallic salts and carbonates are mixed with an earthy paste of ochre or clay and gum, which acts as a medium carrying the copper, silver and bismuth. It is then fired again at about 600°C. At peak temperature reduction must take place for a period of up to half an hour, after which the kiln should be sealed and cooled. The smoke-discoloured paste is cleaned off the ware with a mild abrasive to reveal the lustrous colour.

Lustre pigments				
China clay		100	100	
Red clay	100			
Ochre				100
Carbonate of copper		30		
Carbonate of silver	1¼	2		
Sulphide of copper	25		50	35
Sulphide of silver				12

Lustres for oxidising firing, more suitable for electric kilns, have the metallic salts combined in the form of resinates and an oily medium, which when burnt produces carbon to reduce the metal. These can be purchased ready prepared from suppliers and only require painting on in the technique of enamels.

Glaze tests and faults in firing

Glaze tests can be made on any scraps of biscuit, but it is best to do it systematically and to mark all samples. Small shallow dishes, about 3 inches round can be made quickly and glazed on the inside only, reserving the underside for marking. A bowl shape will test the glaze for flow and contain the latter should it be excessive. Only a 100 grams of materials need be used; these could be mixed in a small mortar, water added, ground if necessary with a pestle, brushed through a sieve and then poured into the bowl, swilled around and drained away to give the correct thickness.

Crazing. This refers to the fine cracks in glaze which may appear after firing, showing that the coefficient of expansion and contraction between the materials is not the same. Fired clay and glaze have a similar co-efficient, so this trouble need not occur, but some oxides do have a higher rate of expansion and contraction under heat than others, namely; soda, potash, barium and lime, in that order. Alkaline glazes are therefore liable to crazing. Lead and magnesia have a lower rate and alumina and silica still less, so that the remedy is to use more of the oxides with lower ratios. In high temperature glazes this means less felspar.

Delayed crazing is often caused by the body being underfired and porous; this allows moisture to get into the biscuit and to expand it causing the glaze to be stretched. The remedy in this case is to harden the biscuit. Crazing does not occur so much on a vitrified body.

Flaking. This is the opposite of crazing and it occurs when the glaze is under compression and is too big for the body, causing it to flake off the body along edges and rims. It is a less common fault and matt or hard glazes are more liable to be affected.

The remedy is also the reverse of crazing, by adding a flux which has a high rate of expansion and contraction. Decreasing the flint or using more felspar, greatly assists.

Crawling. When this occurs, it appears that the glaze has shrunk during the firing, leaving bald patches on the pot and droplets of glaze on the kiln shelves. Glazes containing too much clay or colemanite can do this and the remedy is to use calcined clay and to avoid materials with too much shrinkage. Often it is the result of dusty or dirty biscuit or when the glaze has been re-wetted in some way before firing. Painting on the unfired glaze and wax treatments can disturb the glaze and it sometimes occurs over underglaze painting where the colour has been applied too thickly. Too much polish or smoothing of the clay before firing can cause a rejection of the glaze by the body.

Remedial action of cleaning and slightly roughening the surface and avoiding re-wetting usually cures this fault if care is taken in handling the glazed piece before firing.

Pits and pinholes. These are sometimes caused by tiny pits in the surface of the pot which may have been made by scraping or turning

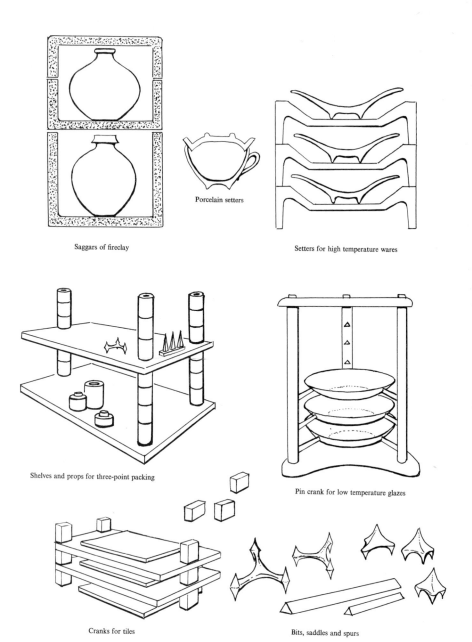

Saggars of fireclay

Porcelain setters

Setters for high temperature wares

Shelves and props for three-point packing

Pin crank for low temperature glazes

Cranks for tiles

Bits, saddles and spurs

21. Kiln furniture

of the pot or by a lack of finish. When the glaze is applied over this surface air becomes trapped in the tiny pores which break or blow during firing, leaving unfilled holes. A little glaze rubbed into such pits before the coating of glaze goes on usually deals with this defect.

Other pitting of the glaze is caused when the glaze boils during the firing, giving off gases which erupt as tiny volcanoes, leaving miniature craters on the surface of the glaze. Glazes made from materials containing fluorine may be so affected due to volatilization of gases and if applied too thickly or underfired, the craters so formed cannot flatten out.

Refiring at a slightly higher temperature can sometimes put this right, but the real cure is to apply the glaze more thinly and to use a longer firing cycle. Underfiring of the glaze is a common cause of unattractive surfaces, and the correct thickness of each individual glaze can be best acquired by testing and experience.

Kiln packing and firing control

The firing of clay into the biscuit state presents few problems. Clay wares should be as dry as possible and the firing done slowly on account of the combined water in the clay, which is driven off as steam until the wares are red hot, after which the clay particles begin to fuse together, the wares can be stacked together and supported, if needs be, in silica sand or alumina.

Glaze firing is another matter, for complete glazing of the pot means that it will stick to the shelf or saggar supporting it, and as it cannot be air-borne, it must either be balanced on sharp, three-pointed supports called stilts, or the glaze must be wiped off the foot or wherever it stands or touches. In the case of porcelain and some stonewares, stilting cannot be used as the wares soften at the high temperature and warp on the triangular stilts. Flat support must be given and an anti-stick used on the shelf or saggar, in the form of a non-fusible bat-wash or alumina.

Firing control is usually done by a pyrometer or pyrometric cones, sometimes by an actual test piece withdrawn while still hot. Pyrometers are electrical instruments constructed on the principle of a thermo-couple connected to a scale showing the temperature recorded.

Cones are tall, triangular pyramids about $2\frac{1}{2}$ inches high. Some smaller ones are made of refractory materials calculated to fuse and bend over at certain heats. Invented by Dr. Hermann Seger in 1866, they bear his name, but are also made under other names with

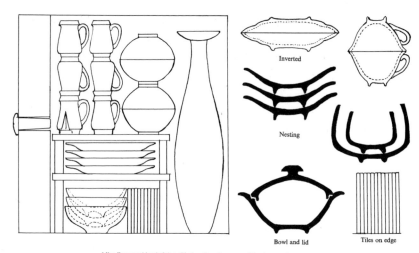

Inverted

Nesting

Bowl and lid

Tiles on edge

Miscellaneous biscuit-firing. Placing the clay ware without supports.

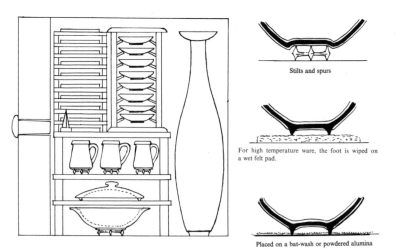

Stilts and spurs

For high temperature ware, the foot is wiped on a wet felt pad.

Placed on a bat-wash or powdered alumina

Miscellaneous glaze firing with or without stilts.

22. Kiln packing

differing numbers and bending temperatures. They cover all temperatures from about 600°C., in upward increases of 20–25°C.

The cones are placed in the kiln where they can be observed through a spy-hole during the firing and in practice it is usual to place three in a row. The middle number will be the one indicating the temperature at which the kiln is to be fired, while the collapse of the low number will give warning of the near climax, the highest number should remain erect to show that the temperature has not been passed. Cones indicate the work done by heat on the materials of their composition and they should be protected from flames and draughts otherwise a false reading of the general temperature of the kiln is given.

A temperature rise of 150°C., per hour is considered to be an appropriate rate and a slower advance means more work done by the heat with a possible collapse of the cones at lower temperature.

Pyrometric cones: standard Seger and American Orton

Seger and Orton cones are calibrated to collapse according to the work done by the heat when the temperature rises at a rate of about 150°C., per hour. If a slower rate is used, they tend to collapse at lower temperatures (consult manufacturer's data).

Seger Cone	Temp. Cent.	Orton Cone	Seger Cone	Temp. Cent.	Orton Cone	Seger Cone	Temp. Cent.	Orton Cone
	600	022		923	09	2a	1150	
	614	021	09a	935			1154	1
	635	020	08a	955	08		1162	2
	683	019	07a	970			1168	3
019	685			984	07	3a	1170	
018	705		06a	990			1186	4
	717	018		999	06	4a	1195	
017	730		05a	1000			1196	5
	747	017	04a	1025		5a	1215	
016	755			1046	05		1222	6
015a	780		03a	1055		6a	1240	7
	792	016		1060	04	7	1260	
	804	015	02a	1085			1263	8
	838	014		1101	03	8	1280	9
	852	013	01a	1105		9	1300	
	884	012		1120	02		1305	10
	895	011	1a	1125		10	1320	
	905	010		1137	01	11	1340	

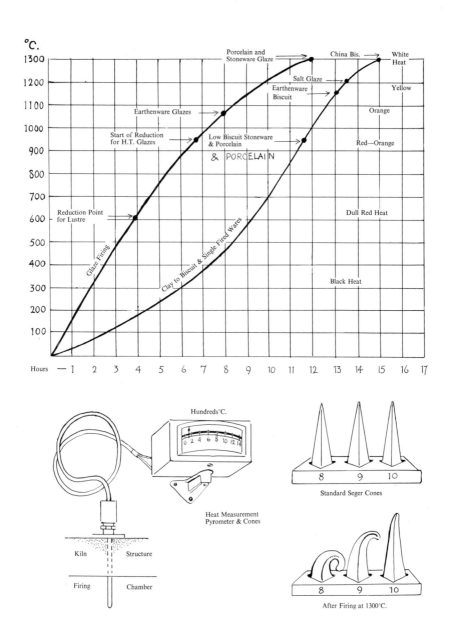

°C.

1300 — Porcelain and Stoneware Glaze → • China Bis. → • White Heat

1200 — Salt Glaze → • Earthenware Biscuit → • Yellow

1100 — Earthenware Glazes → • Orange

1000 —

900 — Start of Reduction for H.T. Glazes → • Low Biscuit Stoneware & Porcelain → • Red—Orange

& PORCELAIN

800 —

700 —

600 — Reduction Point for Lustre → • Dull Red Heat

500 —

400 — Glaze Firing

300 — Clay to Biscuit & Single Fired Wares — Black Heat

200 —

100 —

Hours — 1 2 3 4 5 6 7 8 9 10 11 12 13 14 15 16 17

Hundreds °C.

0 2 4 6 8 10 12 14

Heat Measurement
Pyrometer & Cones

Kiln   Structure

Firing   Chamber

Standard Seger Cones

8   9   10

After Firing at 1300°C.

8   9   10

23. Guide to time and temperatures,
firing of glazes and clay

Appendix I
Atomic weights of the elements used in ceramics

For the purposes of this work, the nearest whole numbers may be used.

Element	Symbol	At.Wt.	Element	Symbol	At.Wt.
Aluminium	Al	26·98	Manganese	Mn	54·93
Antimony	Sb	121·75	Nickel	Ni	58·71
Barium	Ba	137·34	Nitrogen	N	14·00
Bismuth	Bi	208·98	Oxygen	O	15·99
Boron	B	10·81	Phosphorus	P	30·97
Cadmium	Cd	112·40	Platinum	Pt	195·09
Calcium	Ca	40·08	Potassium	K	39·10
Carbon	C	12·01	Selenium	Se	78·96
Chlorine	Cl	35·45	Silicon	Si	28·08
Chromium	Cr	51·99	Silver	Ag	107·86
Cobalt	Co	58·93	Sodium	Na	22·98
Copper	Cu	63·54	Strontium	Sr	87·62
Fluorine	F	18·99	Sulphur	S	32·06
Gold	Au	196·96	Tin	Sn	118·69
Hydrogen	H	1·00	Titanium	Ti	47·90
Iridium	Ir	192·22	Uranium	U	238·02
Iron	Fe	55·84	Vanadium	V	50·94
Lead	Pb	207·20	Zinc	Zn	65·37
Lithium	Li	6·94	Zirconium	Zr	91·22
Magnesium	Mg	24·30			

Appendix II

Pottery compounds, minerals, oxides

The column under 'Equivalent Weight' (Eq.Wt.), is used in glazes as the molecular weight when it represents one molecule of a substance which has two or more molecules of the oxide to be used in the glaze, e.g.: white lead has a formula $2PbCO_3\ Pb(OH)_2$ Mol.Wt. 776. This is divided by the number of lead oxides included which is 3 to give the Eq. Wt. 258. In nearly all cases the Eq. Wt. of the substance is the same as the Mol.Wt. The few exceptions are given in the column Eq.Wt.

Compound		Mol. Wt.	Eq. Wt.	Remarks
Albite	$Na_2O.\ Al_2O_3.\ 6SiO_2$	524		Soda-felspar
Alumina	Al_2O_3	102		
Anorthite	$CaO.\ Al_2O_3.\ 2SiO_2$	278·6		Lime-felspar
Antimony oxide	Sb_2O_3	291·5		White to yellow
Antimoniate of lead	$Pb_3(SbO_4)_2$	993		Yellow
Anatase	TiO_2	80		White
Barium oxide	BaO	153·4		Basic flux
Barium carbonate	$BaCO_3$	197·4		Flux, high temps.
Bentonite				Fine clay. 2%–3% suspends glazes
Bone ash	$Ca_3(PO_4)_2$	310·3	103	Calcium phosphate
Borax	$Na_2O.\ 2B_2O_3.\ 10H_2O$	382		Soluble acid and base
Boracic acid	$B_2O_3.\ 3H_2O$	124		⎫ Soluble
Boric oxide	B_2O_3	70		⎭
Boro-calcite ⎫				Provides insoluble
Calcium borate ⎬	$2CaO.\ 3B_2O_3.\ 5H_2O$	412	206	B_2O_3. Natural fritt
Colemanite ⎭				Secondary flux
Calcium carbonate	$CaCO_3$	100		Flux whiting
Calcium oxide	CaO	56		Flux
Carbon dioxide	CO_2	44		Poisonous
Carbon monoxide	CO	28		Poisonous
China clay	$Al_2O_3.\ 2SiO_2.\ 2H_2O$	258		Source of alumina for glazes
Chromium oxide	Cr_2O_3	152		Green, yellow, red
Cobalt oxide	Co_3O_4	241		Blue
Copper oxide	CuO	79·57		Green, turquoise; red if reduced
Copper carbonate	$CuCO_3$	123·6		
Cornish stone ⎫	$0·30\ CaO$			
	$1·10\ Al_2O_3$			
(average) ⎬	$0·36\ K_2O$	667		
	$8·10\ SiO_2$			
⎭	$0·34\ Na_2O$			
Cryolite	Na_3AlF_6	210	420	Sodium-aluminium fluoride
Dolomite	$CaCO_3\ MgCO_3$	184		
Felspar (potash)	$K_2O.\ Al_2O_3.\ 6SiO_2$	556		Natural fritt
Felspar (soda)				See albite
Felspar (lime)				See anorthite

Compound		Mol. Wt.	Eq. Wt.	Remarks
Flint	SiO_2	60		Silica
Fireclay				Refractory clay
Ferric oxide	Fe_2O_3	160		Iron compounds
Ferrous oxide	FeO	71·8		Cream, brown
Ferroso-ferric ox.	Fe_3O_4	231·4		Celadons, reduced
Galena	PbS	239·3		Lead sulphide
Ilmenite	$FeO.TiO_2$	151·74		Iron-titanium
Lead bisilicate	$PbO. 2SiO_2$	343·6		Fritted lead
Lead monosilicate	$PbO. SiO_2$	283·3		Fritted lead
Lead sequisilicate	$2PbO. 3SiO_2$	626·9	313	Fritted lead
Lead carbonate	$2PbCO_3. Pb(OH)_2$	776	258	Used in fritts
Lead oxide (red)	Pb_3O_4	685·6	223	Used in fritts
Lead oxide	PbO	223		Used in fritts
Lithium carbonate	Li_2CO_3	74		Active flux
Magnesium oxide	MgO	40·3		Flux
Magnesium carb.	$MgCO_3$	84·3		Flux
Manganese carb.	$MnCO_3$	114·93		Brown and
Manganese dioxide	MnO_2	87		purple, flux
Nepheline syenite (average)	$0·25 K_2O \quad 1·10 Al_2O_3$ $0·75 Na_2O \quad 4·65 SiO_2$	462		Lower melting point than fels.
Nickel oxide	NiO	74·7		
Potassium carb.	K_2CO_3	138		Soluble alkaline
Quartz	SiO_2	60		Silica
Rutile	TiO_2	80		Ox. titanium, texture
Soda ash	Na_2CO_3	106		Soluble flux
Sodium carb.	Na_2CO_3	106		Soluble. flux
Sodium oxide	Na_2O	62		Soluble
Sodium silicate	Na_2SiO_3	122·1		Soluble
Spodumene	$Li_2O. Al_2O_3. 4SiO_2$	372		Flux, active
Talc (magnesium silicate)	$3MgO. 4SiO_2. H_2O$	378·96		Secondary flux
Tin oxide	SnO_2	150·7		White, opacifier
Titanium oxide	TiO_2	80		White, semi-matt
Uranium oxide (depleted)	U_3O_8	842		Red in soft glazes yellow at high temps.
Vanadium pentoxide	V_2O_5	181·9		Colouring agent for various effects
Whiting	$CaCO_3$	100		Flux
Zinc oxide	ZnO	81·3		Flux, active at high temps.
Zirconium oxide	ZrO_2	123·2		Opacifier

Appendix III

Glaze recipes, tested on various clays and bodies shown in percentage quantities

No. 1 Glaze Temp. 900°C.
Lead sesquisilicate   83
China clay   17
The high lead content and low temperature of this glaze makes it suitable for a red glaze, produced by adding: 1 to 3 parts of potassium bichromate, or 2 to 7 parts of uranium oxide.

No. 2 Glaze Temp. 950°C.
Potash felspar   14·5
Lead sesquisilicate   74·5
China clay   10·0
Flint   1·0
A harder glaze, useful for general purposes at the above temperature or a little higher.

No. 3 Glaze Temp. 950 to 1050°C.
Wenger's alkaline fritt 1455   85
Whiting   5
China clay   10
Copper carbonate 1 to 3 parts per 100 of glaze.
On a white clay or body, this gives the characteristic alkaline blue.

No. 4 Glaze Temp. 1050 to 1080°C.
Wenger's lead sesquisilicate
1454   78
China clay   13
Flint   9
A good shiny glaze, with typical colour responses from lead.

No. 5 Glaze Temp. 1050 to 1080°C.
Wenger's borax fritt 1457   87
China clay   7
Flint   6
A good glaze for painted white earthenware as the colours remain true.

No. 6 Glaze Temp. 1060°C.
Lead sesquisilicate   52
Whiting   5
Zinc oxide   10
China clay   24
Flint   9
A slightly creamy glaze on white earthenware and red body. The colours produced are good yellows and browns.

No. 7 Glaze Temp. 1080°C.
Lead sesquisilicate   55
Whiting   10
China clay   5
Potash felspar   30
A good general purpose glaze for earthenware.

No. 8 Glaze Temp. 1080°C.
Lead sesquisilicate   55
Cornish stone   15
Whiting   5
China clay   10
Flint   15
A hard transparent glaze due to the use of Cornish stone.

No. 9 Glaze Leadless. Temp. 1080°C.

Potash felspar	16·0
Colemanite	39·5
Whiting	12·5
Zinc oxide	6·0
China clay	11·5
Flint	14·5

A good rich glaze typical of the colemanite content.

No. 10 Glaze Temp. 1080 to 1100°C.

Wenger's alkaline fritt 1455	60
Wenger's borax fritt 1457	30
China clay	10

A double-fritt glaze with added china clay. A good blue-green is produced with the addition of 3 parts copper carbonate, and a rich brown with 5 parts manganese oxide.

No. 11 Glaze Temp. 1120 to 1140°C.

Soda felspar	4·55
Potash felspar	20·50
Lead sesquisilicate	21·00
Whiting	13·50
Colemanite	10·50
China clay	20·50
Flint	9·45

A good clear glaze.

No. 12 Glaze Leadless. Temp. 1150 to 1160°C.

Wenger's alkaline fritt 1455	28·2
Potash felspar	37·3
Whiting	2·0
Barium carbonate	26·2
China clay	4·3
Flint	2·0

A matt glaze results at this temperature, due to the high barium content.

No. 13 Glaze Leadless. Temp. 1160°C.

Wenger's alkaline fritt 1455	13·5
Potash felspar	37·0
Whiting	3·0
Colemanite	23·5
China clay	7·0
Flint	16·0

A transparent glaze with slight opalescence. Alkaline colour responses are especially good from copper.

No 14 Glaze Matt. Temp. 1200°C

Potash felspar	51·0
Whiting	15·5
Barium carbonate	12·0
China clay	16·0
Flint	5·5

A smooth matt surface, with colour responses typical of the lime, barium, potash bases and the high alumina content.

No 15. Glaze Matt. Temp. 1200°C

Colemanite	13·5
Potash felspar	54·5
Whiting	9·5
Barium carbonate	13·0
China clay	5·5
Flint	4·0

The barium, lime and potash bases give strong colour responses.

No. 16 Glaze Semi-matt. Temp. 1200°C.

Colemanite	11·0
Nepheline syenite	40·5
Whiting	8·0
Barium carbonate	10·5
China clay	7·0
Flint	23·0

A similar glaze to No. 15, but nepheline syenite replaces the potash felspar.

No. 17 Glaze Matt Temp. 1230°C.

Nepheline syenite	76
Whiting	16
China clay	4
Flint	4

An opaque matt glaze on stoneware bodies. Colour responses are good for blues and greens. Yellow will result with the addition of vanadium oxide.

No. 18 Glaze Semi-matt Temp. 1230 to 1250°C

Potash felspar	70
Whiting	8
Barium carbonate	10
China clay	7
Flint	5

Strong colour responses typical of the barium, lime and potash bases.

No. 19 Glaze Celadon Temp. 1300°C

Whiting	14·0
Potash felspar	19·0
Soda felspar	18·4
Barium carbonate	4·0
China clay	14·6
Flint	30·0

For celadon add 2–3 parts of iron oxide and fire in a strongly reducing atmosphere on a stoneware or porcelain body.

No. 20 Glaze Matt (Cream) Temp. 1300°C.

Potash felspar	56·0
Whiting	23·4
China clay	20·6

On a stoneware body this glaze can be made white and opaque by the addition of 5 parts of titanium oxide; for an oatmeal colour add 5 parts of rutile.

No. 21 Glaze Bright and shiny. Temp. 1300°C.

Potash felspar	72
Whiting	13
China clay	7
Flint	8

For celadon, add 2 to 4 parts of iron oxide. For rust to black add 5 to 12 parts of iron oxide. For yellow to smoky blue add 5 parts of vanadium oxide. A reducing fire is needed for all the above.

No. 22 Glaze Semi-matt white. Temp. 1300°C.

Cornish stone	80
Whiting	15
Tin oxide	5

A very hard glaze on stoneware or porcelain, strong cobalt responses.

No. 23 Glaze Stoneware. Temp. 1300°C.

Cornish stone	35
Potash felspar	35
Whiting	11
China clay	5
Flint	6
Tin oxide	4
Rutile	4

The rutile gives broken colour effects. Other oxides may be added.

No. 24 Glaze Copper red. Temp. 1300°C.

Potash felspar	35·5
Whiting	14·0
Borax (calcined)	10·0
Flint	37·0
Tin oxide	2·0
Bentonite	1·0
Copper carbonate	0·5

Slight reduction is required and some protection from open flame.

Suppliers of glaze materials, clays, kilns and equipment

All materials, tools and equipment
Wengers Ltd., Etruria, Stoke-on-Trent, Staffordshire
Podmore & Sons Ltd., Shelton. Stoke-on-Trent, Staffordshire

Clays and materials
Harrison Mayer Ltd., Phoenix Works, Hanley, Stoke-on-Trent
Potclays Ltd., Wharf House, Copeland St., Stoke-on-Trent
Moira Pottery Co. Ltd., Burton-on-Trent
Watts, Blake, Bearne & Co. Ltd., Newton Abbot, Devon

Kiln furniture, saggars, shelves and props, etc.
Acme Marls Ltd., Clough St., Hanley, Stoke-on-Trent

Castable refractory concrete
John G. Stein & Co. Ltd., Bonnybridge, Scotland
Lafarge Aluminous Cement Co. Ltd., 73 Brook St., London, W.1.

Overseas Agents & Distributors in New Zealand
Smith & Smith Ltd., PO. Box 2196, Wellington
PO. Box 709, Auckland
PO. Box 22496, Christchurch

U.S.A. Suppliers
United Clay Mines Corp., 101 Oakland Street, Trenton 6, N.J. (clays).
Stewart Clay Co. Inc., 133 Mulberry Street, New York (clays).
A.D. Alpine Inc., 353 Coral Circle, El Seqindo, Cal. 90245 (kilns, etc.)
Electric Kilns Mftrg. Co., Chester II, Pa.
Denver Pure Clay Co., Denver, Colorado
American Art Clay Co., 4717 West 16th Street, Indianapolis 24, Ind.
House of Ceramics, 2481 Matthews Avenue, Memphis, Tenn.

BIBLIOGRAPHY

A Handbook of Ceramic Calculations. A. Heath Webberly. Stoke-on-Trent.

A Potter's Book. Bernard Leach. Faber and Faber. London.

A Manual for the Potter. William Ruscoe. Academy Editions. London.

Chinese Ceramic Glazes. A. L. Hetherington. Cambridge University Press. London.

Clay and Glazes for the Potter. Daniel Rhodes. Pitman. London.

Elements of Ceramics. F. H. Norton. Addison-Wesley. Massachusetts.

The Glazer's Book. A. B. Searle. Technical Press. London.

Understanding Pottery Glazes. David Green. Faber and Faber. London.

GLOSSARY

Acids and bases	Interact with each other, combining under heat.
Alkalis	Compounds of sodium and potassium, present in some minerals and vegetable ashes. The alkaline earths of lime, magnesia and barium also provide fluxes used in glazes.
Alumina	Acts as an amphoteric substance in glazes. Used alone it will withstand high temperatures. It is a constituent of clay.
Amorphous	Non-crystalline structure.
Amphoteric	Chemically neutral, but may be capable of reacting as acid or base according to the conditions of interaction.
Ashes	Vegetable ashes from trees, plants, etc., which provide fluxes for use in glass and glazes.
Aventurine glaze	A term used to denote the separation of isolated individual crystals or spangles in the amorphous glaze.
Bases	The fluxes, alkalis and alkaline earths etc., which combine under heat with the acid substances.
Ball clay	A plastic secondary clay used in bodies and sometimes glazes to provide the alumina content
Bat	A refractory slab or kiln shelf.
Biscuit	Unglazed fired pottery, whether hard or soft. Sometimes called bisque.
Bleb	A blister or bubble in clay or glaze, due to trapped air or unliberated gases.
Blunge	To mix a slip of clay or glaze.
Body	Mixtures of clay and other materials to provide the body of the pot which supports the glaze.
Bone china	An English type of porcelain containing bone ash.
Borax	A soluble substance used by fritting in glazes, supplies both soda and boric acid. A strong flux.
Bristol glaze	A raw glaze containing zinc.
Calcine	To reduce to a powder by the application of heat.
Casting	Taking impressions in plaster, or by pouring liquid clay into moulds.
Catalyst	A substance which induces chemical reaction but remains unchanged.

88

Celadon	The name given to a type of coloured glaze obtained from iron oxide when reduced at high temperatures.
Chamotte	Powdered clay fired and added to bodies as distinct from grog, which is crushed and ground broken bricks etc.
Chün glaze	A chinese glaze of opalescent lavender colour with red or purple splashes.
Colloidal	Jelly-like, without structure.
Cornish stone	Synonymous for china stone, growan, pegmatite or petunze.
Crackle glaze	Intentional and controlled crazing for a decorative effect.
Crawling	Glaze contraction leaving bald patches of biscuit.
Crazing	Cracks in the glaze, which may be unintentional.
Crystalline	Glazes in which crystals are formed by slow cooling and crystal forming agents.
Cullet	Broken glass.
Damper	A device for opening or closing a chimney to control the airflow.
Deflocculate	The dispersion of particles in a slip by an electrolyte such as sodium silicate or sodium carbonate. This gives fluidity.
Devitrify	Changing from a glassy state to a crystalline one.
Dipping	Immersing pots in glaze or slip.
Drawing	Unpacking the kiln.
Dunting	Cracking of the entire pot, due to rapid cooling, and also sometimes due to rapid heating. Cooling cracks show no opening at the edges, whereas rapid heating cracks show a rough edge.
Earthenware	A name given to all kinds of opaque pottery.
Enamel	Soft opaque glazes and colours are often called enamels.
Engobe	Slip dressings on pottery to change the colour or provide a smoother finish.
Eutectic	A mixture of two or more substances with a definite melting point which may be higher or lower than that of either or both of the substances. Usually the eutectic is the mixture which has the lowest melting point.

Faience	A French name given to earthenware of all kinds. Used in England to denote architectural pottery made in blocks. Derived from tin-glazed earthenware made at Faenza in Italy.
Felspar	A crystalline rock found in granite which when decomposed forms clay. The many varieties of felspar contain basic fluxes, alumina and silica.
Fettling	Trimming and finishing the surface of unfired pottery.
Fireclays	Clays which are found in the geological formations known as the coal measures. They are grey or yellow in the clay state, usually burning to a buff colour and resist fusion below 1500°C.
Firing	The application of heat to pottery.
Flambé glazes	Red or purple glazes produced by the Chinese or Western varieties. The colour is due to copper being fired in a reducing atmosphere.
Flux	A substance which lowers the melting point of another.
Fritting	A pre-melting of soluble (and in some cases poisonous) substances together with insoluble substances to render all insoluble. The hot melted fritt is run out into cold water which shatters the mass into fragments to assist grinding.
Galena	Lead sulphide, once used for glazing brown slipwares.
Gel	To make into a jelly-like consistency.
Glaze	Any impervious glassy coating on the surface of pottery.
Greenware	Unfired ware.
Grog	Fired pottery which has been crushed into various grain sizes. Mixed into clays and bodies it gives texture, reduces shrinking, and decreases plasticity, thus assisting in drying.
Hard paste porcelain	True porcelain of the Chinese, fired at over 1300°C.
Heat work	The combined effect of temperature and the duration of firing.

In-glaze decoration	Applied to the glaze before firing, the colours sink into the glaze during firing.
Iron, oxides of	Give a wide range of colours, depending on the nature of the glaze.
Iridescence	A lustrous effect on glazes.
Jar-mill	A rotating porcelain jar and balls for the grinding of glazes.
Kaolin	The Chinese word (anglicised) for china clay.
Kiln	A furnace or oven for potters, of which there are a great variety; i.e. biscuit oven, glost kiln, enamel kiln, intermittent, or continuous, etc.
Kiln furniture	Shelves, props, stilts, etc., used to support the wares during firing.
Lawn	A screen for sieving, identified by mesh size.
Low solubility	Fritted lead glazes in which not more than 5 per cent of lead oxide is soluble.
Luting	Joining leather-hard clay together by slip and modelling the joints securely.
Lustre	A thin film of metal produced on the surface of pottery giving an iridescent sheen
Majolica	A term applied to earthenware glazed with an opaque glaze usually containing tin oxide. Derived from Majorca it is often applied to Faïence and Delft wares.
Marl	Clays containing a proportion of lime. Low grade fireclay.
Maturing temperature	The finishing temperature necessary to achieve vitrification of a body, or to fuse the glaze sufficiently.
Muffle	The inner lining or wall of a kiln which protects the wares from direct heat or flames.
Natural fritts	Felspars are examples of natural fritts, where the forces of nature have brought together soluble and insoluble substances.
Natural glaze	Certain rare and fusible clays which melt at high temperatures to give a glassy coating on coarse stoneware.
Neutral atmosphere	When the atmosphere in the kiln during firing is balanced between oxidation and reduction.
Oil spots	Lustrous metallic spots, resembling oil spots, in high temperature glazes stained with iron.

Orthoclase	Potash felspar.
Orton cones	Pyrometric cones (American).
Oxidation	A chemical reaction whereby oxygen combines with an element or compound. A plentiful supply of oxygen is essential if the glazes are to be oxidised during firing.
Oxide	An element combined with oxygen.
Parian	A kind of porcelain, mainly consisting of felspar and china clay.
Paste	A term used to denote porcelain body; i.e. hard paste, soft paste.
Pegmatite	Cornish stone.
Peeling	The breaking away of fired glaze due to high compression.
Pitchers	Broken fragments of pottery.
Plasticity	The property of clay and other materials which permit shaping and yet retain the manipulated form.
Plucking	The blemish caused when stilts or supports are broken away from the glazed surface of the ware.
Potash	A word used for potassium oxide or carbonate. It is obtained from minerals or from vegetable ashes.
Pyrometer	A device for measuring the temperature within the kiln.
Pyroscopes	Cones or bars of ceramic materials which melt at precise temperatures and are used as guides to measure temperatures.
Quartz	A crystalline form of free silica, which can be used as an alternative to flint.
Raku	A type of pottery originally made in Japan for the tea ceremony, using soft lead and borax glazes.
Raw glaze	A glaze which does not contain fritted materials.
Reduction	Firing the kiln with insufficient oxygen to produce a smoky atmosphere of incomplete combustion. The reducing atmosphere will extract oxygen from the metallic compounds, reducing them to the metallic state, thus bringing about the colours of the metals rather than those of the oxides.

Refractory	Resisting fusion by heat.
Resist	Any substance which repels another, such as wax and water.
Rouge flambé	A French term for red glazes achieved by the reduction of copper.
Saddles	Refractory bars, triangular in section, used to support glazed ware during the firing.
Saggar	A refractory box usually made of fireclay in which wares are placed for protection from direct heat during firing.
Salt glaze	A glaze which is formed on stoneware by the volatilization of common salt thrown on to the fire mouths towards the end of the firing. The resulting vapours combine with the body constituents to form a glossy finish to the wares.
Sang de boeuf	Red glaze similar to *rouge flambé*.
Seger cones	Pyrometric cones named after their inventor.
Setting	Placing the wares in the kiln.
Sgraffito	A decorative process consisting of scratching through one layer of coloured slip to a different coloured body.
Sieves	Synonymous with lawns.
Silica	The potters chief acid substance. Insoluble by itself.
Sintering	The process of heating materials until partial fusion takes place.
Slip	A liquid suspension of clay or other materials.
Slip glaze	A glaze made chiefly of clay.
Snakeskin glaze	A decorative effect obtained by a glaze of low expansion which causes it to crack and crawl, due to surface tension.
Soaking	Maintaining a temperature for some time to achieve saturation by heat.
Soft glaze	Low temperature glazes. Easily scratched by steel.
Soluble	Capable of being dissolved in water.
Spit-out	Small craters in a glaze, occurring on decorated wares at the enamel firing stage.
Spurs	Refractory stilts with a single upward point.
Stilts	Refractory triangular supports for glazed ware in the kiln.

Stanniferous glaze	Glaze rendered opaque by tin oxide.
Stoneware	Pottery which is vitrified.
Sucking	When the vapours of lead oxide and other constituents are absorbed by the kiln furniture or other wares.
Suspending agent	Any substance used in the wet glaze to keep the coarser particles in suspension.
Tea dust glaze	An opaque olive green glaze with flecks of iron. A high temperature stoneware glaze of Chinese origin.
Tenmoku	A stoneware glaze stained with iron and reduced, giving a lustrous black with rust colour where it is thin.
Tessha	Another version of an iron-stained stoneware glaze with broken lustrous metallic markings.
Thermal shock	Sudden heating and cooling of ceramics which can cause dunting.
Thermocouple	The part of a pyrometer projecting inside a kiln consisting of two wires of different metals joined together and protected by a ceramic sheath. When the junction is heated the electromotive force is measured on the scale outside the kiln.
Vitreous	Glassy or non-porous.
Viscosity	Resistance of a liquid to movement.
Volatilization	Conversion of a substance into vapour by heat.
Volcanic ash	The ash or lava discharged from volcanoes.